Pork & Sons

Stéphane Reynaud

Pork & Sons

Photographs
Marie-Pierre Morel

Illustrations
José Reis de Matos

Φ

Contents

Granny pig

210

Barbecued Pork

262

A piggy party

280

Vegetables

Wild boar

340

5

Pépé Barbe

MY GRANDFATHER FRANÇOIS BARBE, KNOWN AS 'MILLEZON'

For over 40 years he presided over the village square as butcher—or rather as professor of butchery! Grandpa knew all about animals. Cattle, calves, lambs, pigs: they were his daily life from Monday through to Sunday. Grandpa was on duty summer and winter, eight days a week. He didn't take many vacations, having a tendency to develop allergies the moment he left Saint-Agrève. He missed its good fresh air! But even if he was somewhat unimaginative in his excuses for not leaving his native village even for a few days, he was easily forgiven. Grandpa worked hard and hard workers earn respect.

At the height of the season it took some effort to get up in the morning when you wouldn't be going to bed again until the next day. For Grandpa rose early, very early. He often told me off, in his own typical way, for vainly trying to lie in now and then, and would regularly—and mischievously—charge into my bedroom about seven in the morning, his apron already showing signs of wear, to wake me up. 'Seven o'clock, Stéphane. You can sleep for another two hours!' Thanks very much, Grandpa, for keeping me so well informed about the progress of the clock! But it was summer, and he had to make butter. If you get up after sunrise the butter just won't 'come.' Malicious tongues, undoubtedly envious of the wonderful weather in Saint-Agrève, will tell you that summer there lasts only from August 14 to 15, but I have to protest. Let me assure you that summer in Saint-Agrève lasts at least from August 10 to 15.

In his store Grandpa, who knew everything about animals, would smile gently at the sight of the summer tourists in their lightweight clothes (only between August 10 and 15, of course). He always generous when weighing meat, but somehow managed to sell customers a slicing sausage, a leg of lamb, and six quails when all they'd come in to buy was two slices of lean ham! 'English spoken here, *se habla español*'—no language barrier bothered Grandpa when it came to selling his goods. He had even mastered Barbanto—a version of Esperanto as spoken by Grandpa Barbe which no one else understood. My Grandpa was a superb businessman.

In winter it was a fine sight to see Grandpa braving the snowdrifts in search of the best ox liver, the fattest hog or young calves for veal. At the wheel of his truck, head lowered, cap pulled well down, he was a veritable snow-plow, facing the cold wind of the high plateaux on his way to isolated farms. None of the local council road-workers could compete with him. Once he had reached a farm he had to drink a toast; business can't be done without a glass of wine. However, Grandpa was very fastidious. Drinking from a glass that wasn't crystal clear or bore traces of a previous visitor really made him suffer. Everyone knew that and

Before you read on . . .

*

deliberately teased him. People enjoyed watching Grandpa's mouth twist as he took a deep breath before lifting a dirty glass to his lips. Once the wine had been drunk though, business could begin. Grandpa was worth watching as he chose an animal, a gloomy expression on his face, always finding some fault with it before discussing the price – in old francs, and paying in old francs too. (Francs and then new francs were French currency before the introduction of the euro.) Heaven knows how often the bank manager tried explaining that 1 franc and 100 francs were not the same sum of money, and that writing a check for 100,000 francs when he was paying for a pig worth 1,000 francs was a sure-fire way to make a lot of farmers very rich. On the other hand, when Grandpa offered me 50 francs for an afternoon's work helping him out, my undernourished money-box – a piggy-bank, of course – ended up with only a miserable 5 centimes.

Grandpa didn't take his secrets with him when he retired. He passed on all his butcher's lore to his son René, the worthy inheritor of the Barbanto language. Taking over the store from a character like Grandpa gave my uncle a lot of trouble. Grandpa in retirement was much more tiresome than Grandpa at work, for he didn't go away quietly to enjoy spending the money he had worked hard for, not he. The butcher's trade was his whole life, and right to the end he could be found somewhere in the store, criticizing all kinds of things – new techniques, new rules and regulations – shaking hands with anyone available and repeating, at frequent intervals: 'But what will people say if I'm not here?'

Pigs are no longer slaughtered at the back of the store ... all that has changed today. The sight of pigs parked in the backyard waiting for the fateful moment to deliver up their carcasses is a thing of the past. Modern standards of hygiene mean that animals can no longer be slaughtered on the premises. The theory and practice of butchery in the good old Barbe fashion lost their original savor, and all of a sudden a child no longer had the opportunity to make a pet of a suckling pig and save it from its destiny – although the reality was that once the pet owner's back was turned, the piglet's fate was sealed. But waste not, want not, as they say. An animal is an animal and we don't shed tears over its fate. Although there was my guinea pig Zouzou, a cute little thing, always snuggling up to something nice and soft in my bedroom. February came and with it the school holidays ... Zouzou went to stay with Grandpa and was found frozen to death in a rabbit hutch at 5°F. It was risky for any animal to come near the Barbe butcher's shop, so much so that when a cat went missing in the village Grandpa was the prime suspect. For the record, the real guilty party was Toupie, a rather vampish alley cat who didn't know the meaning of the word modesty and collected lovers all over the place. She had taken up residence in the loft above the shop, so the local toms all went there for a good night out.

Before you read on . . .

Eventually, Grandpa went to chew the fat with the angels and I'm sure no one there makes him follow the Catholic tradition of eating only fish on Fridays. Fish on Grandpa's plate was like closing the store on Sunday – unheard-of. Once Grandpa was gone, René flung himself into his job, heart and soul. Every kind of sausage and other charcuterie went on appearing in the window to tempt all who appreciate good food. So much so that you could hardly pass the Barbe butcher's store without seeming to hear a whisper coming from somewhere very far away, urging you to go in. Grandpa was a real character – even though he's passed on, he's still somewhere in the store.

And now my walking boots and I have been out and about on the high plateaux of the Ardèche – more accurately, in Saint-Agrève – for 38 years. Mum, you were really smart when you decided to be born there among the spruce trees on a bend in the winding road, far from the madding crowd. And a message to my readers: why not visit Saint-Agrève? It's well worth it, for although you have to negotiate sharp bends in the road, you get to breathe clean air at a height of 3,300 feet. Spend some leisurely time here and you'll soon be a Saint-Agrève addict.

And finally, a note about my recipes. People cook differently in different parts of the world due to varying local ingredients and cooking customs. So that you can use the recipes in this book wherever you live, although I have sometimes listed French or other European ingredients (see the back of the book for descriptions of cheeses and wines), I have also included alternative ingredients whenever possible. Even so, some things may be more difficult to find in your local shops than others. In these cases don't be afraid to use a more readily available ingredient instead. If in doubt ask your butcher or grocer for help; they are usually a great source of information and should be able to point you in the right direction. As a result, the flavor of your dish may be slightly different from mine, but that's the beauty of cooking – it's alchemy at it's best!

BOUCHERIE - CHARCUTERIE

Spécialité Ardéchoise de Saucisson et Jambonnettes

R. BARBE

5, place de la République, 5
SAINT - AGRÈVE (Ardèche)

Stéphane

I was very small when Grandpa Barbe sat me on the cold imitation leather of the seat in his truck and took me to visit the local farms. I had some unforgettable experiences there and became familiar with the festive atmosphere when a pig was slaughtered. It is 30 years since I first attended the ceremony and I can say that the tradition has endured. Nothing has really changed, apart from a few details as set out below.

7 YEARS OLD

FIRST PIG-KILLING

10°F outdoor temperature

1 hot chocolate

1 pig, weighing 400 pounds

2 bales of straw

6½ feet of blood sausage

2 slices of bread and butter,
1 hot chocolate

60 cooking sausages

50 cured sausages

1 fricassée,
2 glasses of Arcens mineral water

50 caillettes (Ardèche sausages)

44 pounds pâté

18 pounds roasting pork

2 cured hams

2 pork bellies

40 YEARS OLD

LATEST PIG-KILLING

10°F outdoor temperature

2 glasses of white wine

1 pig, weighing 400 pounds

2 bales of straw

6½ feet of blood sausage

Cheese, pâté,
3 glasses of white wine

60 cooking sausages

50 cured sausages

1 fricassée,
3 glasses of red wine

50 caillettes (Ardèche sausages)

44 pounds pâté

18 pounds roasting pork

2 cured hams

2 pork bellies

*

Before you read on . . .

February,
Saint-Agrève (on the high plateaux of the Ardèche),

5°F, 7.00 a.m.

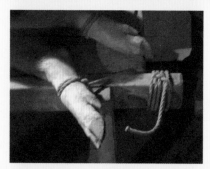
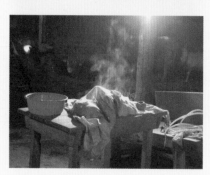

Pig-killing time at Saint-Agrève

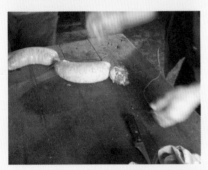

Pig-Killing time at Saint-Agrève

IN PRAISE OF THE PIG

The ritual when a pig is slaughtered still has many good years ahead of it. It is fortunate that the standardization of flavor in today's food industry has not yet reached the Ardèche region, where tradition mounts a good defense. Slaughtering and butchering call for precise organization. The team forms around the slaughterer. He makes incisions, cuts, saws; his assistants bone the meat, cut it up, chop it. The rhythm keeps on going, interrupted only for several glasses of good white wine and a few sausages that would make even the most ardent vegetarian's mouth water.

Eric

ERIC'S PIGS ARE HAPPY PIGS

A pig is very small, about three weeks old, when it goes to stay at Eric's gourmet establishment to indulge in its favorite pastime – eating. Every meal is a porcine banquet, a three-star fattening-up program, with a menu of whey, potatoes, and cabbages. But this happy state of affairs doesn't last for ever, as the aim of the temporary pampering is to produce meat of the best quality, something that Eric does exceptionally well. No stress, plenty of space, lots and lots to eat – the pigs who pig out at his place are sure to tantalize any connoisseur's taste buds.

*

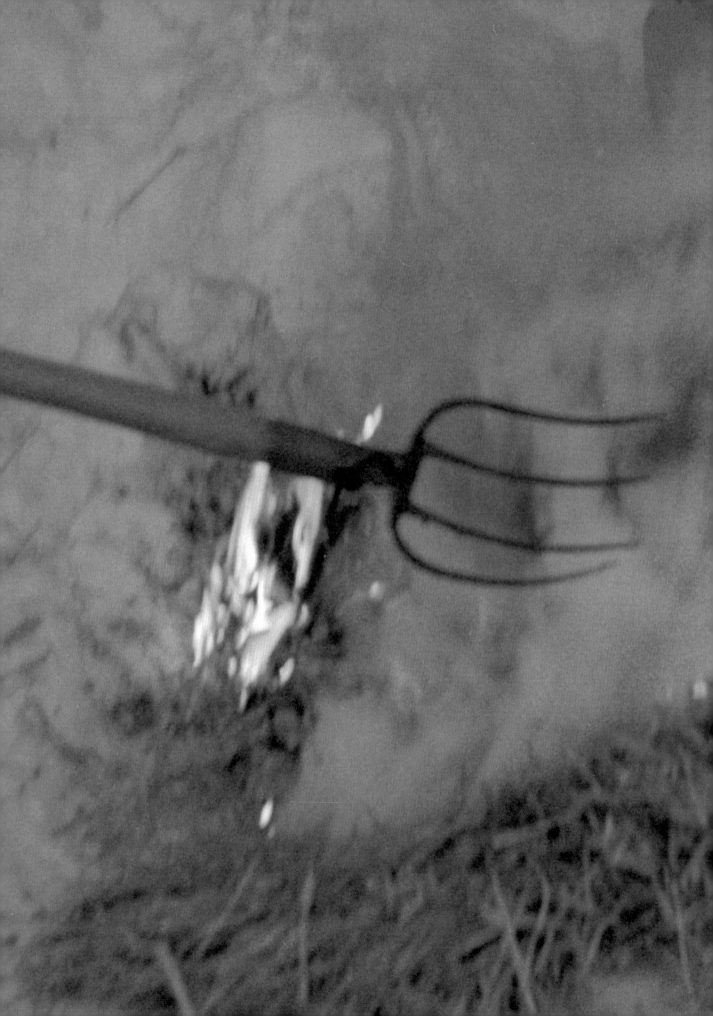

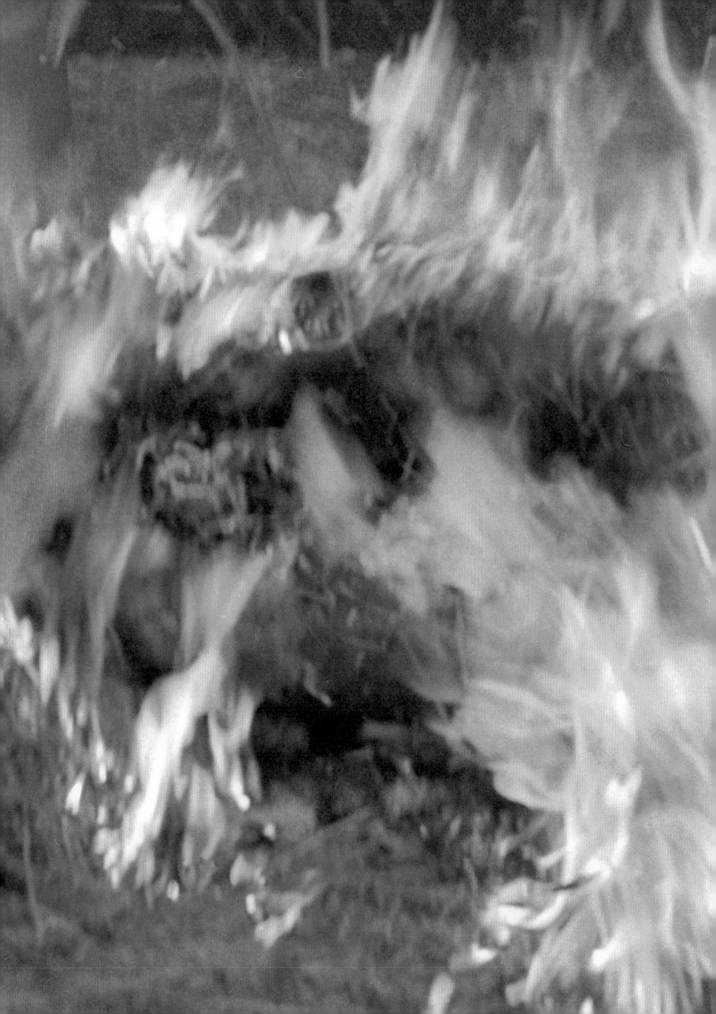

Aimé

AIMÉ LOVINGLY PRACTICES HIS TRADE

Used to making a whole battery of machine tools purr along, Aimé deals
with an animal before you can say 'knife.' Moreover, he has been known
for being sharp as a proverbial knife for several decades on many of the
farms on the high plateaux. The pig family all acknowledge his expertise.
Prince of the art of cutting up the carcass, lord of the blood sausage,
with his surgical skill he can transform a beast weighing 400 pounds into
a charcutier's display window within a morning. Nothing is left to chance
when he has to deal with a mountain of meat, and sausages both large
and small won't wait. Then Aimé turns into something like a Swiss
watchmaker: working precisely, meticulously and fast (that's the only real
difference between him and the Swiss watchmaker), he cuts up the carcass,
frees the caul and intestines, ties roasts, bones the meat, removes fat,
carves, and chops ... all in time to an appreciative clicking of his tongue
as he takes a glass of wine to help him in his labors.

*

For all the family . . .
when it's a big one!

6½ pounds fresh pork fat, preferably leaf lard
6½ pounds onions, finely chopped
4 cups crème fraîche
1¼ cups cognac or brandy
6 pinches of Quatre-épices (see page 154)
2 pinches of sugar
½ cup salt
6¼ quarts fresh or frozen pig's blood (if your
   butcher cannot provide, try an Asian market)
a few yards of sausage casings
generous ½ cup fresh lard

Making
Blood Sausages

Pig-killing time at Saint-Agrève

Heat 2¼ pounds of the fat in a large pan. Add the onions and cook over low heat, stirring occasionally, for about 20 minutes, until very soft.

Dice the remaining fat, mix with the softened onions, and allow to partially melt. Add the crème fraîche, cognac, spice, sugar, and salt. Pour in the blood, stirring constantly to prevent it from congealing.

Using a funnel, gently fill the sausage casings. Cook them in a large pan of gently simmering water (176°F) for 10 minutes.

Remove the blood sausages and grease them using a cloth spread with the lard.

This is a classic blood sausage recipe which you can flavor however you like. Vary the ingredients freely by adding chopped chestnuts, apples, ground allspice, or aniseed...

Remember to check that there are no holes in the sausage casings by inflating them (just as you'd blow up a balloon) before ladling in the mixture.

Blachou and Florette

AN INSEPARABLE COUPLE, ALWAYS AROUND AT A PIG-KILLING

They appear at dawn as if by magic: Blachou with his woolly cap on and a smoking hand-rolled cigarette between his lips; Florette the dog, stomach nicely rounded by years of pig-killings, nose at ground level, taking in the festive atmosphere. They are always ready and willing to join the team, the center of which – the pig – is still dreaming and unaware of its fate, its mind dulled by large quantities of potatoes. For a pig dreams of nothing else, and fattens up even while it's asleep. This sweet vision is only fleeting, however, and there's no time for sentimentality when Blachou goes into action. He calmly bones and cuts up the carcass, while Florette growls and snaps up anything that's going.

*

BREAKING FOR A SNACK AT TEN O'CLOCK

A man without a knife will end up no more than mere skin and bone! Don't forget to bring a knife when you're working with a pig-killing team, so that you can help yourself to a chunk of crusty bread, a slice of sausage, or a piece of Picodon goat cheese.

Pierre and Charlou

BROTHERS WITH DEEP ROOTS
IN SAINT-JEAN-ROURE

These two brothers are the living history of peasant life. Welcome guests
at the pig-killing – they look after us and make sure we don't go thirsty –
Pierre and Charlou are like two oak trees that have been around for ever.
No one can imagine one without the other.

Time has no hold on their peaceful existence – they are no longer just part
of the landscape, they are the landscape.

*

PERUSING THE NEWS AT A PIG-KILLING

A pig-killing gives you the chance to look through the *Dauphiné Libéré* newspaper.
Like the pig itself, the paper is taken apart and devoured: every story is enriched
with pithy comments. Immerse yourself in the *Dauphiné Libéré* and you'll soon
feel you belong on the high plateaux of the Ardèche.

FRICASSEE, A HEARTY STEW FOR LUNCH

This is the time of day when the women, having collected their kids from school, join the men for lunch. Never mind a slimming diet of healthy carrots and steamed fish, they'll enjoy some real cooking for a change. The fricassée is delicious and brings color to everyone's cheeks. It will sustain you through an afternoon of work, and the memory will live on until evening.

A short lesson in anatomy

ham

foot

loin

Picnic ham

Boston butt

Pig-killing time at Saint-Agrève

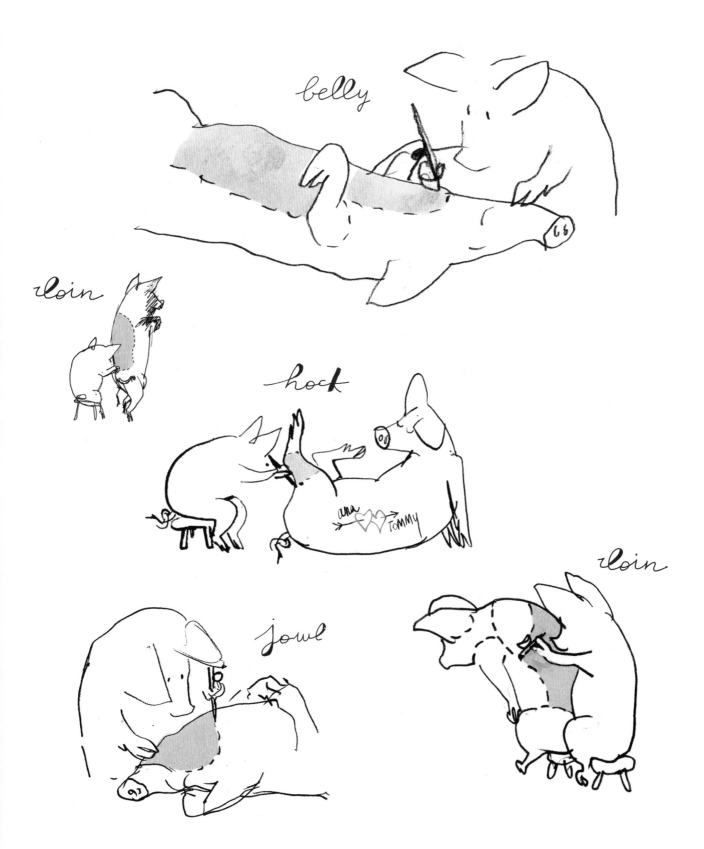

belly

loin

hock

loin

jowl

45

Blood sausage recipes

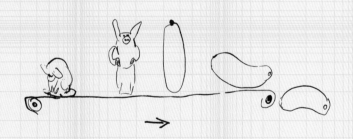

fricassée

PREPARATION TIME: 20 MINUTES
COOKING TIME: 30 MINUTES

SERVES 6

generous ½ cup lard or scant ½ cup sweet butter
2 large onions, thinly sliced
6 waxy potatoes, thinly sliced into rounds
7 ounces pig's liver, cut into cubes
2 pig's kidneys, cut into cubes
7 ounces pig's heart, cut into cubes
1¾ pounds blood sausage (see below), cut into cubes
1 bunch of fresh parsley, chopped
3 garlic cloves, chopped
salt and pepper

Melt the lard or butter in a large pan over low heat. Add the onions and potatoes and cook, stirring gently, for 10–15 minutes, until lightly browned. Stir in the liver, kidneys, and heart and cook until evenly browned. Add the blood sausage and cook until it has heated through, then remove the pan from the heat.

Sprinkle the parsley and garlic over the fricassée, season to taste with salt and pepper, and serve immediately, straight from the pan.

BLOOD SAUSAGE

Blood sausage is also known as boudin noir, blood pudding or black sausage. It is usually sold pre-cooked. In Louisiana it is also called boudin rouge. You can also buy Spanish or Argentinian morcilla or German blutwurst. What you really want is fully cooked Pyrenees-style blood sausage (see *Sources*).

Blood sausage with walnuts and chestnuts

PREPARATION TIME: 5 MINUTES
COOKING TIME: 30 MINUTES

SERVES 6

8 shallots
8 garlic cloves
¾ cup fresh whole milk
3 tablespoons olive oil
¾ cup dry white wine
2 teaspoons beef or veal stock powder,
  dissolved in 2 tablespoons of hot water
14 ounces peeled chestnuts, thawed if frozen
scant 1 cup shelled walnuts
1¼ cups heavy cream
1¾ pounds blood sausage (see page 48)
salt and pepper

Peel the shallots and garlic but leave them whole. Put the garlic in a pan, add the milk, and simmer gently. Heat the olive oil in another pan, add the shallots, and cook, stirring occasionally, for 10–15 minutes, until evenly browned.

Meanwhile, heat the wine in a third pan. Mix the stock with the wine, add to the shallots, and cook until reduced. Drain the garlic and add it to the pan along with the chestnuts and walnuts, then pour in the cream, heat through and season to taste with salt and pepper. The sauce should have a syrupy consistency.

Remove the skin from the blood sausage, cut it in half lengthwise, and cook it in a skillet.

Serve the two blood sausage halves topped with the shallot and nut garnish.

Blood sausage with fall fruits

PREPARATION TIME: 15 MINUTES
COOKING TIME: 30 MINUTES

SERVES 6

6 firm pears
2 pinches of ground cinnamon
3 quinces
scant ½ cup sweet butter
6 small eating apples, preferably flavorful heirlooms
  such as Jonathans or Winesaps
1¾ pounds blood sausage (see page 48)
2 tablespoons sugar
3½ ounces peeled chestnuts in a vacuum pack or jar
2 tablespoons Calvados or applejack
salt and pepper

Peel the pears and coat with the cinnamon. Core the quinces and cut into fourths.

Melt half the butter over very low heat. Add the quinces and cook for 10 minutes, turning occasionally until lightly browned.

Meanwhile, core and halve the apples. Add to the pan along with the pears, and turn to coat.

Melt the remaining butter in a skillet. Remove the skin from the blood sausage, add the blood sausage to the skillet and heat through. Keep warm.

When the fruit starts to soften, add the sugar and chestnuts and cook until caramelized. Add the Calvados and heat for 1 minute, then ignite. When the flames have died down, season to taste with salt and pepper.

Serve the blood sausage accompanied by the three fruits and the flambéed cooking liquid.

Blood sausage gratin
with caramelized onion

PREPARATION TIME: 40 MINUTES
COOKING TIME: 30 MINUTES

SERVES 6

1¾ pounds mealy (baking) potatoes
⅔ cup slightly salted butter
1 teaspoon freshly grated nutmeg
4 tablespoons olive oil
6 onions, sliced
generous ½ cup chopped fresh pork belly or
  lightly cured slab bacon
scant 1 cup shelled hazelnuts
1 bunch of fresh tarragon, chopped
1¾ pounds blood sausage (see page 48)
2 slices of toast, crumbled
salt and pepper

Cook the potatoes in a large pan of lightly salted boiling water for 15–20 minutes, until tender.
Drain well, mash with a fork, and beat in the butter and nutmeg. Season to taste with salt and pepper.

Meanwhile, heat the olive oil in a large pan. Add the onions and cook over low heat, stirring
occasionally, for 20 minutes, until very soft. Stir in the pork belly and hazelnuts and cook, stirring
frequently, until browned. Add the tarragon.

Preheat the oven to 350°F.

Remove the skin from the blood sausage and cut it into ½-inch slices. Cook in a skillet, turning
occasionally, until caramelized.

Place half the mashed potatoes in a gratin dish and cover with all the onions. Place the blood sausage
slices on top and cover with the remaining mashed potatoes.

Sprinkle with the toast crumbs and bake in the oven until the topping is golden brown.

Blood sausage, apple, potato, and fennel tart

PREPARATION TIME: 50 MINUTES
COOKING TIME: 20 MINUTES

SERVES 6

3 shallots, thinly sliced
4 tablespoons crème fraîche
3 tablespoons olive oil, plus extra for drizzling
4 waxy potatoes
2 eating apples
generous ½ cup chopped smoked bacon
14 ounces blood sausage (see page 48)
12 ounces puff pastry dough, thawed if frozen
all-purpose flour, for dusting
¼ fennel bulb, thinly sliced
1 bunch of arugula, optional, torn into pieces
salt and pepper

Combine the shallots and crème fraîche in a bowl. Add 1 tablespoon of the olive oil and season with salt and pepper. Set aside.

Cook the potatoes in lightly salted boiling water for 15–20 minutes, until tender. Drain well, then cut into thin rounds. Preheat the broiler.

Peel, core, and slice the apples. Heat the remaining olive oil in a skillet, add the apple slices, and cook until they are just beginning to color.

Spread out the bacon on a cookie sheet and cook under the broiler, turning once, for 5–8 minutes, until tender. Meanwhile, remove the skin from the blood sausage and cut the sausage into thin slices.

Preheat the oven to 350°F.

Roll out the puff pastry dough on a lightly floured surface to a 10-inch round and place on a cookie sheet. Spread 2 tablespoons of the shallot cream evenly over the dough round. Sprinkle with the fennel and lardons, then arrange alternate layers of blood sausage, potato, and apple slices on top. Cover with the remaining shallot cream. Bake in the oven for 20 minutes.

Sprinkle the tart with the arugula, if using, drizzle with olive oil, and serve immediately.

Blood sausage crostini with pears and beet

PREPARATION TIME: 30 MINUTES
TO ASSEMBLE: 10 MINUTES

MAKES 12

6 tablespoons olive oil
2 garlic cloves, coarsely chopped
3 pears
1½ teaspoons sweet butter
12 slices of rustic bread
7 ounces blood sausage (see page 48),
  cut into ¼-inch slices
1 cooked beet, cut into thin batons
fresh chives, to garnish

Heat the olive oil in a skillet. Add the garlic and cook until it is just beginning to color. Remove the garlic with a slotted spoon and discard. Set aside the pan of flavored olive oil.

Peel and core the pears, then cut each into eighths. Melt the butter in another skillet, add the pears, and cook over low heat, turning occasionally, until golden brown.

Heat the garlic-flavored olive oil, add the bread slices, in batches, and cook until golden brown on both sides. Drain on paper towels.

Meanwhile, cook the slices of blood sausage in another pan until lightly browned on both sides.

Divide the pieces of pear, the beet batons, and blood sausage slices among the slices of fried bread and garnish with the chives.

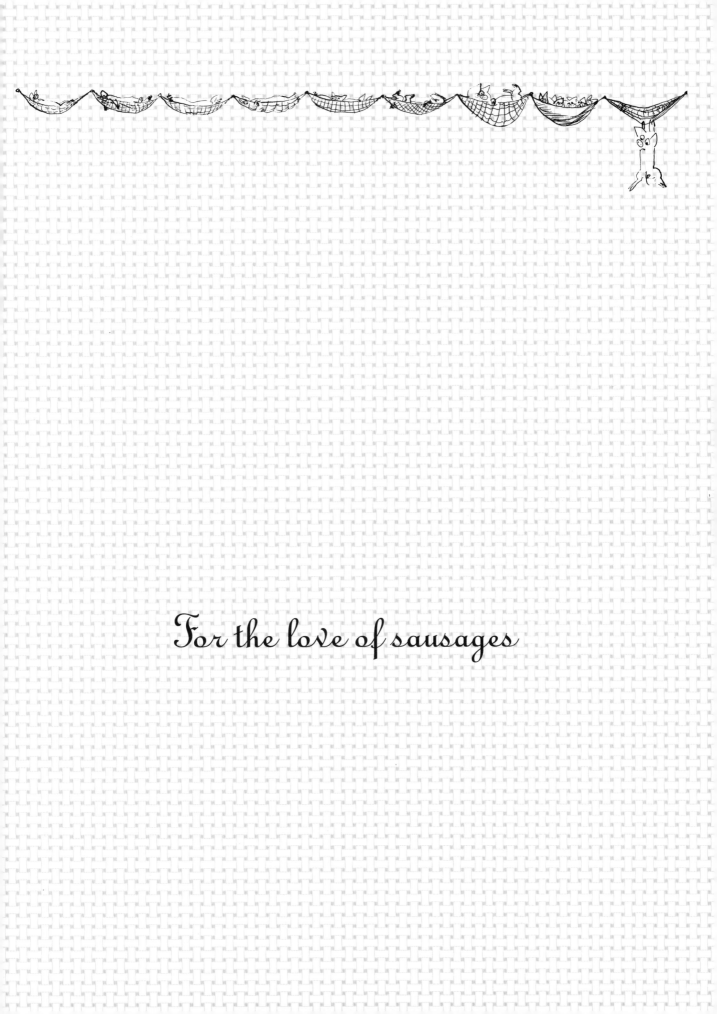

For the love of sausages

SAUSAGES

WHAT ARE THEY?

A fresh sausage is a meat-filled casing. The casing is traditionally made from an intestine and it is filled with a mixture of finely or coarsely chopped meat, including both fat and lean meat, and seasoned to taste. Seasoning is particularly important in making sausages. The word sausage – and its French equivalents *saucisse* and *saucisson* – is ultimately derived from the Latin *salsus*, meaning 'salted.'

DO YOU SPEAK SAUSAGE?

Many regions throughout France have their own sausage recipes and the sausages, in turn, take their names from these regions. From Savoy to Toulouse sausages and from Strasbourg *knack* to Montbéliard *saucisse*, sausage is named in the same way as cheese. Its identity is locked into its region, giving it a distinctive shape and character: spiced or smoked, coarse or fine, plain or herb-flavored, mixed with other meats or consisting solely of pork, it is a tribute to the pork butcher's skill.

Of course, sausages are not only an icon of French gastronomy, as most other countries have their own culinary traditions too.

Germany alone has over 1,500 varieties of *Wurst*, including the famous Frankfurter, known to all fans of hot dogs and a real transatlantic star.

The great British breakfast would not be complete without the aroma of broiled sausages, and the famous Spanish *chorizo* sets international taste buds tingling with its peppery seasoning. Italy and Hungary produce fabulous salami too...

It would take an encyclopedia in several volumes to cover all the different kinds of sausages and their local names in detail. In the United States, the government does not allow meats to be stored above 42°F, so most traditional curing methods are illegal. However, some cured sausages are now imported. Please see *Sources* (at the back of the book) for finding these meats in major US cities and by mail order and the internet. Always call your butcher first because many of these meats are available only by special order.

Making
small sausages

Making large
slicing sausages

63

THREE TYPES OF SAUSAGES

SAUSAGES FOR BROILING OR GRILLING

Godiveaux	Small casing, 8 inches long, fine texture
Chipolata	Small casing, 8 inches long, fine texture, often flavored with herbs
Paysanne	Medium casing, 6 inches long, coarse texture
Toulouse	Medium casing, 6 inches long, fine texture

✳

SAUSAGES FOR POACHING

Paysanne	Medium casing, 6 inches long, coarse texture
Frankfurter	Small casing, 6 inches long, smooth texture, can be smoked
Strasbourg	Small.casing, 6 inches long, smooth texture, may contain beef, often colored red
Saveloy or Cervelas	Large casing, 10 inches long, fine texture, may contain truffles and pistachios, served in slices
Montbéliard	Small casing, 6 inches long, fine texture, flavored with cumin and shallots, smoked
Morteau	Large casing, 10 inches long, coarse texture, smoked, secured with twine

✳

SAUSAGES FOR SPREADING

Strichtwurscht (Liverwurst)	Large casing, 6 inches long, fine texture often with pig's liver (Lewerwurscht), flavored with cumin and paprika, smoked
Soubressade	Large beef casing, fine stuffing with large pieces, often flavored with pepper

✳

For the love of sausages

Toulouse sausages

Montbéliard

Morteau,
the genuine version

Gendarmes

'Snout'

Strichtwurscht

Frankfurter sausages

Sausages for poaching

Saucisse paysanne

CURED SAUSAGES

'How do you get to be a cured sausage?', asked one of the usual cooking variety, not yet wrinkled by maturing.

Large cured sausages for slicing, the equivalent of Italian salami, are very popular because they are so easy to keep and serve. As they are rich in proteins and lipids, they are ideal for snacks.

MAKING CURED SAUSAGES

Cured sausages are made in the same way as cooking sausages. The natural intestines of the pig are used as casings and filled with a mixture of fat and lean pork. Then they are cured. Unlike cooking sausages, the slicing sausage develops its character through malo-lactic fermentation, which is sometimes encouraged by drying at 77°F for 24 hours. The process of transformation then begins. Once removed from the drying room, the sausage naturally develops microorganisms which help its flavors to become concentrated.

MATURING AND DRYING

The maturing and drying stage is very important. The rate at which water evaporates from the sausage has to be checked regularly to prevent a crust from forming. This happens when evaporation is too fast and is a problem because the crust will prevent the remaining water from evaporating. On the other hand, evaporation that is too slow creates a sticky formation on the surface, which also prevents the rest of the water from evaporating.

Cured sausages develop and mature rather like a good wine. Depending on the shape and size of the sausage, drying lasts from five to eight weeks, but the length of the process is largely determined by the consumer's taste. The sausage-maker's finances also play a role as the shorter the maturing period, the heavier the sausage will be. Cured sausages, once matured, will have lost 20 percent of their original weight.

ANDOUILLE, ANDOUILLETTE, VIRE

The huge sausage family contains other kinds too, including andouille and andouillette. These are cooked sausages basically consisting of pig chitterlings, usually smoked and then dried. The best known come from Vire in Normandy and Guémené in Brittany. The basis of andouillettes is pig's tripe and intestines, cooked and then filled into a casing. And then there are Danish and Hungarian salami, Italian mortadella ... French andouille is not to be confused with Cajun-style andouille, which is a heavily smoked, richly flavored, and very spicy pork sausage used in hearty dishes such as jambalaya and gumbo.

✳

Jésus — a large pork sausage from Franche-Comté

LARGE CURED REGIONAL SAUSAGES

Rosette   Casing known as 'rosette' with a spindle shape, 16–20 inches long, 1¾–2½ pounds, medium texture, dried for 8 weeks

Jésus   Casing known as *sac de porc*, 12 inches long, thick, 2–3 pounds, medium texture, dried for 8–10 weeks

Saucisson   Chaudin, 8–10 inches long, texture often coarse, 11 ounces–1 pound 2 ounces, dried for 6 weeks

Saucisse sèche   Also know as Lorraine, long casing, 20 inches, medium texture, U shape, dried for 2–3 weeks

Salami   Chaudin, fine and relatively fat texture, 1¾–3¼ pounds, can be cooked or dried

Mortadella   Large synthetic casing, smooth texture, cooked with pieces of fat, can be matured with wine, flavored with pistachios and coriander seeds, 2¼–225 pounds

Chorizo   Long or large casing, U shape or large sausage, medium texture, enhanced with paprika and garlic. Not to be confused with Mexican choritzo, which is a very spicy, raw sausage

*

Coppa

Salami

Lorraine

Andouille de Guémené

Andouille de Vire

Lomo

Cacciatori

Chorizo

General purpose

Sausage recipes

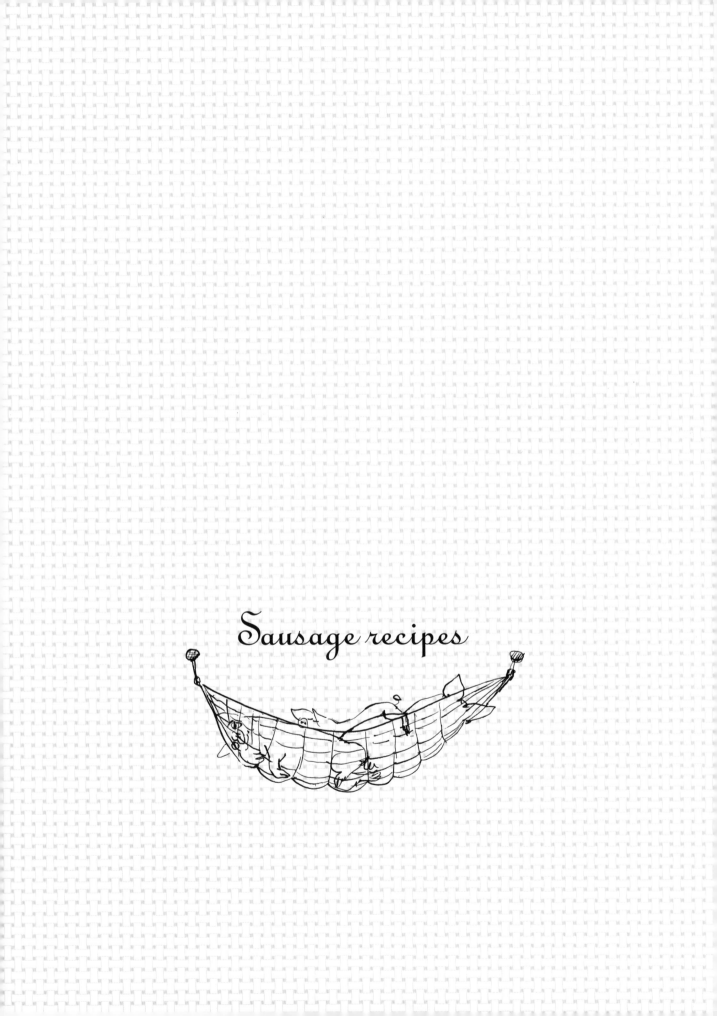

Sausage cassoulet

SOAKING TIME: 24 HOURS
PREPARATION TIME: 15 MINUTES
COOKING TIME: 4 HOURS

SERVES 6

2 cups dried navy beans, soaked in cold water
  for 24 hours and drained
1 onion
1 carrot
3 garlic cloves
2 bay leaves
1 tablespoon glace de veau
6 ripe tomatoes, quartered
3½ ounces fresh pork rind, sliced
4 cups dry white wine
6 Toulouse or paysanne sausages (see pages 64 and 65), or
  country-style link sausages, such as saucissons à l'ail (see *Sources*)
2 slices of toast, crumbled
generous ½ cup duck fat, melted

Bring a pan of water to simmering point and add the beans, onion, carrot, garlic, and bay leaves. Simmer for 2 hours, then drain, and reserve the cooking liquid. Discard the flavorings. Stir the glace de veau into the cooking liquid and add the tomatoes. Preheat the oven to 325°F.

Place the beans in a terracotta dish and add the pork rind. Pour in the white wine and enough of the reserved cooking liquid and tomatoes almost to fill the dish. Prick the sausages and push them down into the mixture. Bake in the oven for 2 hours, adding more of the cooking liquid and tomatoes if necessary to prevent the mixture from drying out. Before serving preheat the broiler. Sprinkle the cassoulet with the toast crumbs, pour the melted duck fat over them, and broil briefly.

CASSOULET

Cassoulet is a rich, slow-cooked bean stew containing meat (usually pork sausages, pork, goose and duck), and white haricot beans.

For the love of sausages

Sausage confit with split peas

PREPARATION TIME: 10 MINUTES
COOKING TIME: 2½ HOURS

SERVES 6

2¼ cups split peas
1 onion
1 leek
1 bunch of fresh cilantro
3 fresh thyme sprigs
1 large saucisse de couennes or other rind sausage
   such as Cotechino, Zampone, or Musetto (see *Sources*)
1 tablespoon glace de veau
scant 1 cup heavy cream

Bring a large pan of water to simmering point. Add the split peas, onion, leek, cilantro, and thyme and cook for 1 hour. Add the sausage and glace de veau and simmer for 1 hour more.

Drain the peas but leave the sausage in the cooking liquid. Place the peas in a flameproof casserole, strain in enough of the cooking liquid to cover, add the sausage, and pour in the cream. Cook over very low heat for about 30 minutes.

Split open the sausage lengthwise and serve straight from the casserole. The sausagemeat should be served with a spoon.

Montbéliard sausage gratin and vegetable tian with thyme

PREPARATION TIME: 20 MINUTES
COOKING TIME: 1 HOUR

SERVES 6

2 eggplants, cut into thin rounds
6 tomatoes, cut into thin rounds
4 zucchini, cut into thin rounds
3 large onions, cut into thin rounds
6 fresh thyme sprigs, leaves only
4 bay leaves
6 garlic cloves, coarsely chopped
¾ cup white wine
scant ½ cup olive oil
4½ teaspoons sweet butter
6 Montbéliard sausages (see pages 64 and 65) or other
  small smoked sausages flavored with cumin, such as
  smoked Mexican–American-style choritzo (see *Sources*)
sea salt

Preheat the oven to 325°F.

Place all the vegetable rounds vertically, in layers, in a casserole. Add the thyme leaves, bay leaves, garlic, white wine, olive oil and butter. Prick the sausages and arrange them on the top.

Cover and bake in the oven for 1 hour, until the vegetables are very tender. Season with sea salt and serve.

For the love of sausages

Warm sausage and Puy lentil salad with herb marinade

PREPARATION TIME: 25 MINUTES
COOKING TIME: 40 MINUTES

SERVES 6

2¼ cups green lentils, preferably French ones from Puy
1 bouquet garni
2 uncooked link sausages, such as sweet Italian sausages or saucissons à l'ail (see *Sources*)
⅓ cup smoked slab bacon, cut into thin batons
1 teaspoon Dijon mustard
a dash of balsamic vinegar
scant ½ cup walnut oil
1 shallot, chopped
3 fresh tarragon sprigs

FOR THE MARINADE

scant ½ cup walnut oil
6 fresh chives, finely chopped
2 fresh tarragon sprigs, finely chopped
1 shallot, finely chopped
1 tablespoon chopped hazelnuts

Combine all the marinade ingredients in a bowl and set aside until required.

Place the lentils, bouquet garni, and sausages in a pan and add plenty of water. Simmer over low heat for 40 minutes.

Meanwhile, preheat the broiler. Spread out the bacon on a cookie sheet and broil, turning once, until golden.

Make a vinaigrette by mixing together the mustard, balsamic vinegar, walnut oil, and broiled lardons.

Remove the sausages from the pan and slice. Discard the bouquet garni. Drain and rinse the lentils, place in a bowl, and add the vinaigrette, shallot, and tarragon.

Place a dome of lentils in the center of each serving plate, surround with the slices of warm sausage and coat with the marinade. Serve immediately.

Sausage in brioche

PREPARATION TIME: 20 MINUTES PLUS 30 MINUTES FOR RISING
COOKING TIME: 40 MINUTES

SERVES 6

4 eggs
2¾ cups all-purpose flour
2 teaspoons baking powder
scant 1 cup heavy cream
scant ½ cup fresh whole milk
½ cup shelled pistachio nuts
⅓ cup unsmoked slab bacon, cut into batons and broiled
1 summer sausage or cervelas (see page 64)

Beat the eggs in a bowl until thoroughly combined. Sift the flour with the baking powder into another bowl, then gradually beat in the eggs, and pour in the cream and milk to make a smooth dough. Mix the pistachios and bacon into the dough.

Half-fill a nonstick loaf pan with the dough, place the sausage along the center, and cover with the remaining dough. Let rise in a warm place for 30 minutes.

Meanwhile, preheat the oven to 400°F.

Bake the loaf in the oven for 40 minutes. Turn out onto a wire rack to cool.

Serve in slices with a well-seasoned frisée salad.

For the love of sausages

Sabodet with Mâcon wine, vegetables and dried mushrooms

PREPARATION TIME: 40 MINUTES
COOKING TIME: 40 MINUTES

SERVE 6

1 cup dried porcini mushrooms
4 fresh parsley sprigs
3 garlic cloves
2 shallots, chopped
6 carrots, cut into cubes
6 young turnips, cut into fourths
½ celery root, cut into cubes
7 ounces cremini mushrooms
1 Sabodet or other large rind sausage such as
  Cotechino, Zampone, or Musetto (see *Sources*)
2¼ cups white Mâcon wine or any young
  French Burgundy (Chardonnay)

Place the dried mushrooms in a bowl, add warm water to cover, and let soak for 25–30 minutes. Meanwhile, remove the leaves from the parsley sprigs and reserve the stalks. Chop 1 of the garlic cloves with the parsley leaves. Drain the mushrooms and cook them in a skillet with the parsley and garlic mixture.

Place the shallots, carrots, turnips, celery root, cremini mushrooms, porcini mushroom mixture, parsley stalks, and remaining garlic cloves in a flameproof casserole. Add the sausage and pour in the white wine. Cover and cook over low heat for 40 minutes.

Skim off any fat from the surface with a ladle and then serve straight from the casserole.

SABODET AND MÂCON

A speciality of Lyon, sabodet sausages are pork sausages made from pig's head and skin. They have a strong, earthy flavor. Mâcon wines are red and white wines from the Mâconnais part of Burgundy, France.

For the love of sausages

Warm Morteau sausage with Roseval potato, carrot and celery salad

PREPARATION TIME: 30 MINUTES
COOKING TIME: 40 MINUTES

SERVES 6

2 Morteau sausages (see pages 64 and 65)
  or other large smoked sausages
6 Roseval or other red-skinned potatoes, unpeeled
1 carrot, halved lengthwise
1 celery stalk, cut into thin batons
1 shallot, finely chopped
1 tablespoon balsamic vinegar
scant ½ cup olive oil

Place the sausages in a pan of water, bring to a boil, and simmer for 20 minutes. Add the potatoes to the pan, bring back to a boil, and simmer for a further 20 minutes.

Meanwhile, cut the carrot into thin strips using a vegetable peeler. Combine the carrot, celery, and shallot in a bowl. Whisk together the olive oil and balsamic vinegar in a pitcher, then pour about half the dressing over the vegetables, and toss lightly.

Drain the potatoes and sausages and cut them into rounds. Arrange them on serving plates, cover with the vegetable mixture, and add a drizzle of vinaigrette to the potatoes.

For the love of sausages

Morteau sausage and smoked bacon with fresh salsify and shallot

PREPARATION TIME: 20 MINUTES
COOKING TIME: 40 MINUTES

SERVES 6

2 Morteau sausages (see pages 64 and 65)
  or other large smoked sausages
6 pear shallots or other elongated shallots
olive oil, for drizzling
juice of 1 lemon
2¼ pounds salsify
¼ cup slightly salted butter
1 tablespoon sugar
2¼ cups beef stock
6 slices of smoked bacon

Poach the Morteau or other large smoked sausages in gently simmering water for 40 minutes.

Meanwhile, preheat the oven to 350°F.

Place the shallots in an ovenproof dish, drizzle with olive oil, and bake for 20 minutes, until they feel springy to the touch.

Stir the lemon juice into a bowl of water. Working on one root at a time, peel the salsify, cut it into even short lengths, and immediately place it in the acidulated water to prevent discoloration. Drain the salsify, place in a sauté pan, add the butter, sugar, and beef stock, and pour in enough water to cover.

Meanwhile, preheat the broiler.

Cook the salsify over low heat until it is glazed and shiny golden brown. Broil the bacon for 2–4 minutes on each side, until lightly browned.

Drain the sausages and slice. Make a bed of salsify on six individual serving plates. Cover with the sliced sausages, the bacon, and, finally, the shallots split open lengthwise. Spoon over the salsify cooking juices and serve.

Andouille and dandelion salad

PREPARATION TIME: 10 MINUTES

SERVES 6

scant ½ cup olive oil
2 garlic cloves, chopped
1 tablespoon cider vinegar
1 teaspoon honey
2½ cups dandelion leaves
24 slices of Vire andouille sausage (see pages 66 and 69)
  or any other tripe sausage such as Spanish butifarra
  (see *Sources*); do not use Cajun andouille

Heat the olive oil in a small skillet. Add the garlic and cook briefly, then remove the skillet from the heat. Stir in the vinegar and honey.

Wash the dandelion leaves and spin or pat dry. Place in a bowl and toss with the warm vinaigrette.

Make a small bed of dandelion leaves on each of six serving plates and top with a slice of sausage. Continue making layers in this way until all the ingredients are used up, then serve.

Broiled Guémené andouille sausage with vegetable mirepoix

PREPARATION TIME: 30 MINUTES
COOKING TIME: 20 MINUTES

SERVES 6

½ cup olive oil
2 garlic cloves, chopped
2-inch piece of fresh ginger root, chopped
4 very ripe tomatoes, cut into fourths
1 teaspoon tomato ketchup
3 shallots, chopped
1 celery root, diced
2 eggplants, diced
2 zucchini, diced
2 onions, sliced
18 thick slices of Guémené andouille sausage (see pages 66 and 69)
  or any other tripe sausage such as Spanish butifarra (see *Sources*);
  do not use Cajun andouille

Heat 2 tablespoons of the olive oil in a pan. Add the garlic and ginger and cook, stirring frequently, for a few minutes. Add the tomatoes and cook over low heat, stirring occasionally, for about 20 minutes, until pulpy. Stir in the ketchup, transfer the mixture to a food processor, and process to a thick and smooth coulis. Preheat the broiler.

Heat 4 tablespoons of the remaining oil in a large pan. Add the shallots and celery root and cook, stirring occasionally, for about 10 minutes, then add the eggplants, cook for a few minutes more, then add the zucchini. Cook until the vegetables are tender crisp. Meanwhile, heat the remaining oil in another pan and cook the sliced onions, stirring occasionally, for 5–10 minutes. Broil the slices of andouille or other tripe sausage. To serve, form a dome of the vegetables on individual serving plates, top with alternating slices of sausage and fried onions, and garnish with the tomato coulis.

MIREPOIX

This is a classic preparation of basic ingredients (onions, carrots, celery, and sometimes herbs), usually diced. Mirepoix can be eaten raw, but is often sautéed in butter and used as the flavor base for sauces, soups and stews or as a bed on which to cook meat or fish.

For the love of sausages

Herb-marinated sausage

PREPARATION TIME: 5 MINUTES
MARINATING TIME: 1 WEEK

SERVES 1 AS AN APPETIZER

1 mature cured sausage of your choice, such as saucisson
   (see pages 64 and 65) or soppressata (see *Sources*)
1 garlic clove
10 juniper berries
2 fresh thyme sprigs
1 bay leaf
a pinch of fresh rosemary
1¼–2½ cups olive oil
toasted bread, to serve

Slice the sausage and remove the skin. Place the sausage slices in a preserving jar with the garlic, juniper berries, thyme, bay leaf and rosemary. Add olive oil to cover, close the lid, and leave in the refrigerator for at least 1 week.

Serve the sausage with a slice of toasted bread.

chorizo and mozzarella tapas

PREPARATION TIME: 10 MINUTES
COOKING TIME: 5 MINUTES

MAKES 10

2 slices of toast, crumbled
100 g (3½ oz) ground almonds
2 eggs
10 small mozzarella cheese balls
10 fresh basil leaves
10 thin slices of spicy, dry Spanish chorizo sausage
   (see pages 68 and 69) or fresh spicy Mexican sausage
   (see *Sources*), cooked and drained
oil, for deep-frying

Mix together the toast crumbs and ground almonds in a shallow dish. Beat the eggs well in another shallow dish. Roll the mozzarella cheeses first in the egg and then in the toast and almond mixture. Repeat this process three times.

Place each mozzarella cheese on a wooden toothpick and add a basil leaf and a slice of chorizo.

Heat the oil in a large pan, add the tapas and fry for 15 seconds. Drain well and serve warm.

For the love of sausages

grilled chorizo and fresh herb salad

PREPARATION TIME: 15 MINUTES
COOKING TIME: 5 MINUTES

SERVES 6

1 bunch of fresh chervil
1 bunch of fresh tarragon
1 bunch of fresh cilantro
1 bunch of fresh flat-leaf parsley
1 bunch of arugula
1 handful of wild dandelion or escarole leaves
12 slices of dry Spanish chorizo sausage
  (see pages 68 and 69), cut into thin batons
2 tablespoons wine vinegar
6 tablespoons canola oil
2 red onions, thinly sliced into rings

Coarsely tear the herb leaves from their stalks and mix them with the salad greens in a bowl. Heat a griddle pan, add the chorizo, and cook for a few minutes. Stir the wine vinegar into the cooking juices.

Add the oil to the salad and toss lightly. Add the chorizo and cooking juices and garnish with the onion rings.

For the love of sausages

Chorizo tortilla

PREPARATION TIME: 20 MINUTES
COOKING TIME: 20 MINUTES

SERVES 6

½ cup olive oil, plus extra for brushing
1 pounds 5 ounces small potatoes, cut into large cubes
7 ounces dry Spanish chorizo sausage (see pages 68 and 69),
  cut into strips, or ½ pound Mexican chorizo (see *Sources*),
  cooked, drained, and cut into chunks
3 onions, sliced
5 eggs
scant ½ cup heavy cream

Preheat the oven to 250°F. Brush an ovenproof dish with oil.

Heat 5 tablespoons of the olive oil in a skillet. Add the potatoes and cook over medium heat for about 8 minutes, until just beginning to color. Meanwhile, heat the remaining oil in another pan. Add the chorizo and onions and cook over low heat, stirring occasionally, for 5 minutes, until the onions have softened. Combine the onions, chorizo, and potatoes. Beat the eggs until foaming, then add the cream.

Spoon the chorizo mixture into the prepared dish and pour over the beaten eggs to cover. Bake in the oven for 15–20 minutes, until golden brown and cooked through. Test by inserting the point of a sharp knife – it should come out dry. You could also make several smaller tortillas, as pictured, but you will need to reduce the cooking time.

For the love of sausages

Hamming it up

A little more ham, if you please!

COOKED HAM

A KIND OF HAM MISHMASH

From the traditional French ham sandwich to the ground ham given to tiny children, every French citizen eats an average 11 pounds of cooked ham a year. Its nutritional benefits – rich in iron and potassium, low in fats for a pork product – and its versatility make it a permanent resident in all self-respecting refrigerators.

Cooked ham is made from the hind legs of the pig, which can be boned and molded to shape, trimmed of fat and skinned, cured in brine, and slow-cooked by a variety of techniques. French stores sell three kinds of cooked ham; 'superior' cooked ham is prepared without phosphates or gelling agents. Your butcher will also sell several varieties. Ask his advice if you need to find an alternative for any of the following recipes.

DISTINGUISHING BETWEEN FRENCH SUPERIOR HAMS

When ham cooked on the bone is called York ham or Prague ham, the name does not refer to the place where it was produced, but to its method of preparation and cooking.

Braised ham	Ham that has been slowly cooked.
Au torchon	Ham boned and cooked in broth (cooked in a cloth).
Ardennes ham	A pear-shaped ham.
Jambon de Paris	Can be recognized by its rectangular shape. (Not all jambon de Paris is of superior quality, so make sure you ask your butcher for the best he has.)
'Choice' ham	Boned and molded ham made without gelling agents.
'Standard' ham	Boned and molded ham made with some additives not permitted in the others.

'Snout'

DRY-CURED HAMS

The food of kings in the ancient world, dry-cured hams have made ham a real star, ennobling the art of charcuterie. Their high reputation is the outcome of very careful work in rearing pigs and producing ham. You don't get good hams without good pigs. The choice of breed and the way the animals are fattened are essential to producing high-quality hams. Uncooked ham is prepared by dry-salting the surface of the haunch. This salting, often done by hand, dries out the meat to improve its keeping quality. It is at this point that some producers add aromatic herbs and spices to give the ham flavor.

The hams are then put in special drying rooms where ventilation, temperature, and humidity are carefully controlled so that the ham can mature in the best possible conditions.

Now the ham begins its process of transformation. The salt permeates the meat and matures it. It turns an intense red and develops its aroma as the process speeds up. The maturing and drying period varies according to the kind of ham; a good dry-cured variety can't be made from just any old ham.

Superior dry-cured ham: matured for a minimum of 210 days.

Dry-cured ham: matured for a minimum of 130 days.

Uncooked ham: matured for less than 130 days.

BAYONNE HAM

Bayonne ham can be produced only in the 22 *départements* of Aquitaine. The pigs, monitored from birth, are fed entirely on cereals and the haunches are rigorously selected before becoming hams. The climate of southwestern France, between the ocean and the Pyrenees and subject to great variations in humidity, is the essential factor in maturing the ham and gives it a succulent texture. Other French hams have made a reputation outside their native country, including Auvergne ham, Savoy ham, Ardennes ham, and Vendée ham.

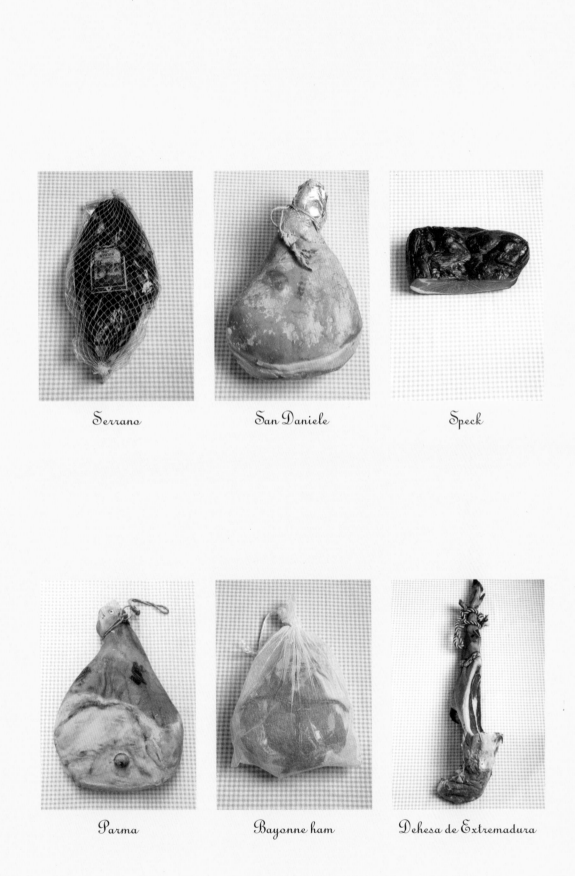

Serrano

San Daniele

Speck

Parma

Bayonne ham

Dehesa de Extremadura

JAMÓN DE CERDO

Serrano ham, produced in Spain, has a worldwide reputation. The name simply refers to the word *sierra*, meaning 'mountain.' In fact, the special quality of Serrano ham is that its production follows the pattern of the mountain climate. The pigs are slaughtered and the meat is cured in winter, then it is dried during a period of changing temperatures as summer approaches, acquiring its characteristic flavor. The specifications for Serrano ham state that it is a traditional specialty subject to certain regulations, but do not guarantee the origin of the pigs or the place where the ham is produced. Spain produces one of the best hams in the world from *pata negra* ('black hoof') pigs. These wonderful hams bear the appellation Iberico and the best Iberico ham is called *bellota*. The word *bellota*, meaning acorn, indicates that the pigs are foraging animals fattened among oak trees, where they feed entirely on acorns, doubling their weight during their time in the forest. The climate – cold winters, hot summers – and the process of maturing for a minimum of 24 months give both the fat and the lean meat of the ham an inimitable texture and aroma.

PROSCIUTTO DI MAIALE

Italy too can claim an ancient tradition in the making of its hams. The quality of Italian ham is recognized and appreciated by all gourmets. Prosciutto di Parma, a real gastronomic treat, results from extremely rigorous expertise and techniques. The breed of pig used is the Large White Landrace or Duroc, weighing at least 350 pounds, born and reared in 11 regions of Italy. The diet selected, the conditions in which it is reared – everything is recorded in specifications that guarantee the high quality of the ham. The particular flavor of prosciutto di Parma comes from the art of the master curers, the heirs to several centuries of experience. They use very little salt, which means that the ham dries more slowly. After 12 months it will finally be revealed whether it is worthy to bear the sign of the ducal crown with its five points, the official guarantee that the meat conforms to specifications. This sign is awarded only after careful checking, a process called *spillatura*. The ham is checked in five specific places to confirm that it has matured successfully.

In northern Italy, prosciutto di San Daniele is made from large pigs weighing 440 pounds, reared exclusively in the Veneto, Piedmont, and Lombardy. San Daniele hams are matured for ten months, so their meat is paler than that from Parma, and the foot is left on the ham. Other hams such as the Bosses ham from the Val d'Aosta complete this rich tradition of charcuterie.

SCHINKEN AND SPECK

Germany, Austria, and Belgium have their own skills in maturing hams too. Their methods may be lesser known, but the end products are certainly of high quality. Ardennes ham, Black Forest ham, and Austrian speck long ago became popular outside their own regions.

Hamming it up

Dry-cured Auvergne ham:
mmm, very good

LABELS DESIGNATING QUALITY

THREE DESIGNATIONS OF QUALITY IN EUROPE TO PROTECT AGRICULTURAL VARIETY AND DEFEND HAMS AGAINST IMITATIONS

PDO

Protected designation of origin guaranteed

Ham produced, developed and matured in a defined geographical area with recognized and confirmed expertise.

Spain
Dehesa de Extremadura
Guijuelo

Jamón de Huelva

Jamón de teruel

Italy
Prosciutto di Carpegna

Prosciutto di Modena

Prosciutto di Parma

Prosciutto di San Daniele

Prosciutto di Veneto Berico-Euganeo

Prosciutto Toscano

Valle d'Aosta Jambon de Bosses

Valle d'Aosta Lard d'Arnad

Speck dell'Alto Adige

Portugal
Presunto de Barrancos

IGP

Protected geographical indication

Ham linked to a regional area at one stage of production, development or maturing.

Germany
Ammerländer-Dielenrauchschinken-Katenschinken

Ammerländer-Schinken-Knochenschinken
Schwarzwälder Schinken

Austria
Tiroler Speck

Belgium
Ardennes ham

France
Bayonne ham

Ardennes ham

Italy
Prosciutto di Norcia

Portugal
Presunto de Barroso

STG

Traditional speciality

Ham made in a traditional manner (development, rearing of the pig).

Spain
Serrano

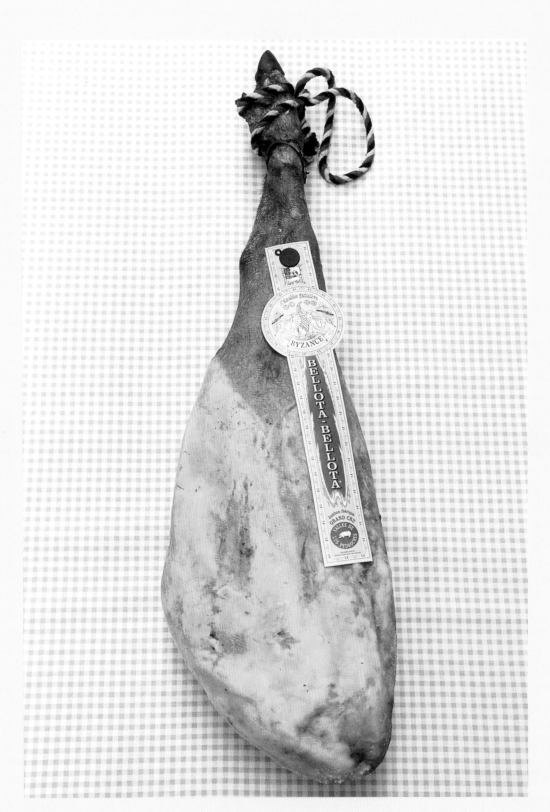

Iberico de Bellota

Ham recipes

Prosciutto, arugula, and Parmesan Crostini

PREPARATION TIME: 20 MINUTES

MAKES 10

6–7 tablespoons olive oil
10 slices of day-old rustic bread
1 bunch of arugula
2 ounces Parmesan cheese
5 very thin slices of prosciutto or other dry-cured ham,
  halved lengthwise
coarsely ground black pepper

Heat half the oil in a skillet. Add the bread, in batches, and fry on both sides until golden, adding more oil as necessary. Drain well on paper towels. Place the arugula in a bowl and drizzle with a little oil. Using a vegetable peeler, cut the Parmesan into shavings.

Place a half slice of ham on a board, top with a little arugula and Parmesan, season with pepper, and roll up like a tortilla wrap. Repeat with the remaining ham, arugula, and Parmesan. Arrange the wraps on the fried bread and serve.

Bayonne ham with toasted nuts and piquillo peppers

PREPARATION TIME: 20 MINUTES

MAKES 10

½ cup pine nuts
4 tablespoons olive oil
10 slices of baguette
1 bunch of fresh cilantro
10 canned piquillo peppers, drained
5 thin slices of Bayonne (see pages 104 and 105)
  or other dry-cured ham, such as prosciutto, halved

Dry-fry the pine nuts in a small skillet, stirring frequently, for about 2 minutes, until golden, then transfer to a plate. Heat the oil in a large skillet, add the baguette slices, in batches, and fry on both sides until golden. Sprinkle them with half the cilantro leaves. Stuff each pepper with pine nuts and most of the remaining cilantro.

Place a pepper on each piece of fried bread, cover with a half slice of ham, and sprinkle with the remaining cilantro leaves.

PIQUILLO PEPPERS

Piquillo are sweet red peppers traditionally grown in northern Spain. The peppers are roasted, giving them a rich, spicy flavor, then peeled and packed in jars. You could use regular roasted small red peppers instead.

Ham, Appenzeller cheese and dried apricot Crostini

PREPARATION TIME: 20 MINUTES

MAKES 10

5 ready-to-eat dried apricots, thinly sliced
¾ ounce Saint-Moret whipped cream cheese
  or mild chèvre
1 teaspoon maple syrup
5 slices of whole-wheat bread, halved
2 ounces Appenzeller or other semi-hard mature cheese
5 slices of speck (see pages 105 and 106) or other
  dry-cured ham, such as prosciutto, cut into strips
coarsely ground black pepper

Mix one-third of the dried apricots with the cream cheese and maple syrup in a bowl.

Spread this mixture thickly on one side of each half slice of bread. Using a vegetable peeler, cut thin shavings of Appenzeller or other semi-hard cheese. Sprinkle the cheese shavings, remaining dried apricots, and strips of ham over the bread and season with pepper, or with freshly cut chives if you prefer.

Hamming it up

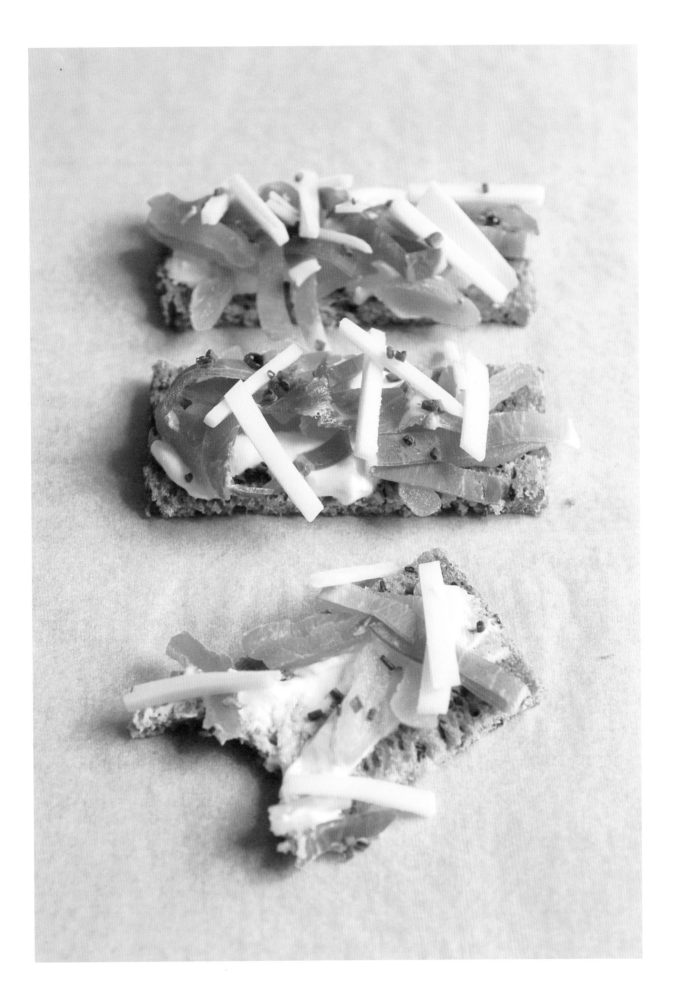

Serrano ham, Sun-dried tomato and basil crostini

PREPARATION TIME: 20 MINUTES

MAKES 10

1 bunch of fresh basil
3½ ounces sun-dried tomatoes in oil,
  drained and cut into fourths
6 tablespoons olive oil
3 garlic cloves, sliced
10 slices of baguette
5 slices of Serrano ham (see pages 105 and 106) or
  other dry-cured ham, such as prosciutto, halved

Chop the basil, reserving ten whole leaves for the garnish. Set aside ten pieces of tomato. Crush the remaining tomatoes with 1 tablespoon of the olive oil and the chopped basil in a mortar with a pestle. If necessary, add a little of the oil from the tomato jar to make a purée. Heat the remaining olive oil in a skillet, add the garlic, and cook until crisp and golden. Add the slices of bread, in batches, and cook on both sides until golden. Remove from the pan and drain on paper towels.

Place a little of the tomato purée, a piece of tomato, a half slice of Serrano ham, a basil leaf, and a few garlic slices on each slice of fried bread.

Hamming it up

Jambon de Paris, bacon, apple and curry Sandwiches

PREPARATION TIME: 20 MINUTES

MAKES 16

4 slices of bacon
1 Granny Smith or other tart eating apple
1 celery stalk, cut into thin batons
4 slices of cooked jambon de Paris (see page 102) or
   other unsmoked, fully-cooked ham, coarsely chopped
1 bunch of fresh parsley, chopped
4 pita breads

FOR THE SAUCE

1 egg
scant 1 cup olive oil
1 teaspoon white wine vinegar
1 teaspoon mustard
1 teaspoon honey
1 teaspoon curry powder

Preheat the broiler, then cook the bacon, turning once, for 4–8 minutes. Cut it into small strips. Peel, core, and dice the apple.

To make the sauce, beat the egg in a bowl, then whisk in the oil, 1–2 teaspoons at a time, until about a fourth of it has been absorbed. Beat in the vinegar, then continue to whisk in the oil, adding it in a steady stream. Finally, whisk in the mustard, honey, and curry powder.

Stir the bacon, apple, celery, ham, and parsley into the sauce. Cut each pita bread in half and fill the pockets with the ham mixture. Cut each half in half again and serve.

Hamming it up

jambon de Paris, fig, Comté cheese and dried fruit toasts

PREPARATION TIME: 20 MINUTES

MAKES 10

10 dried figs
1 tablespoon brown sugar
10 slices of multigrain bread
5 slices of cooked jambon de Paris (see page 102)
  or other unsmoked, fully-cooked ham, halved
3½ ounces sharp Comté or Gruyère cheese, sliced
10 shelled hazelnuts
10 shelled almonds
20 fresh chives

Place the figs in a pan and add water to cover. Stir in the sugar and cook over medium–low heat for 5 minutes. Using a slotted spoon, transfer the figs to a blender and process to a fine purée.

Toast the bread on both sides in a toaster or under a preheated broiler. Spread half the fig purée on one side of each toast and top with the ham, cheese, the remaining fig purée, and the nuts. Garnish with the chives.

Hamming it up

Prosciutto and broiled vegetable crostini

PREPARATION TIME: 20 MINUTES

MAKES 10

5 slices of eggplant
6 tablespoons olive oil, plus extra for brushing
2 lengthwise slices of zucchini
10 cherry tomatoes
10 slices of rustic bread
2 fresh thyme sprigs
5 slices of good dry-cured ham, such as prosciutto,
  cut into strips
2 fresh tarragon sprigs
sea salt

Preheat the broiler. Brush the eggplant slices with oil, then broil on both sides until lightly golden. Meanwhile, blanch the zucchini slices in boiling water for 2 minutes, then drain, and broil on both sides until lightly golden.

Heat the olive oil in a skillet, add the tomatoes and slices of bread, in batches, and cook over high heat until the bread is golden brown on both sides. Remove the fried bread and drain on paper towels. Cut all the vegetables into small pieces and sprinkle with thyme leaves.

Place the vegetables and strips of ham on the slices of fried bread. Season with sea salt and garnish with tarragon leaves.

Ham and pickle sandwiches (for jean)

PREPARATION TIME: 10 MINUTES

MAKES 4

3 tablespoons sweet butter, softened
16 cornichons (miniature French cucumber pickles), coarsely chopped
6 fresh chives, coarsely chopped
1 baguette, cut into fourths
4 slices of cooked ham, cut off the bone, such as from a shank portion
ground black pepper

Cream the butter in a bowl, then beat in the cornichons and chives, and season with pepper.

Slice each piece of baguette in half horizontally. Spread the cornichon butter on one half of each baguette fourth. Top with the ham and the other half of the baguette fourth and it is ready to eat.

This simple meal keeps the cornichons crunchy without the problem of later finding them on your lap.

Ham, Emmental, pain d'épice and avocado Sandwiches

PREPARATION TIME: 10 MINUTES

MAKES 20

5 slices of smoked bacon
10 slices of good-quality pain d'épice or other gingerbread
1 avocado
juice of ½ lemon
5 slices jambon de Paris (see page 102) or other unsmoked,
  fully-cooked ham, halved
3½ ounces Emmental cheese, sliced
½ red onion, sliced
salt and pepper

Preheat the broiler. Cook the bacon under the broiler for 2–4 minutes on each side. Toast the pain d'épice on both sides.

Peel and pit the avocado, brush it with the lemon juice, and mash with a fork. Season with salt and pepper.

Cut the toasts in half diagonally and spread one side of each triangle with the avocado purée. Top with the ham, Emmental, bacon, and onion slices.

PAIN D'ÉPICE

Translated as spice bread, pain d'épice can be described as a more savoury version of traditional gingerbread. In addition to ginger, it often includes all or some of the following flavors: cardamom, cloves, nutmeg and rum.

My club sandwich

PREPARATION TIME: 20 MINUTES

MAKES 4

8 slices of dry-cured or unsmoked bacon
8 thin slices of smoked bacon
12 thick slices of white bread
4 slices of jambon de Paris (see page 102)
  or other unsmoked, fully-cooked ham, halved
4 tomatoes, thinly sliced
4 hard-cooked eggs, thinly sliced
1 cucumber, thinly sliced
1 handful of arugula

FOR THE SAUCE

1 egg
1 teaspoon mustard
1 teaspoon white wine vinegar
scant 1 cup peanut oil
1 tablespoon tomato ketchup
Tabasco sauce, to taste
a dash of brandy
salt and pepper

Preheat the broiler. Grill the bacon, turning once, for 5–8 minutes, until cooked through. Toast the bread.

To make the sauce, whisk together the egg, mustard, and vinegar in a bowl and season with salt and pepper. Gradually whisk in the oil, then add the ketchup, a few drops of Tabasco, and a dash of brandy.

Spread the sauce on a slice of toast and top with ham, tomato, unsmoked bacon, hard-cooked egg, smoked bacon, cucumber, and arugula. Add another slice of toast and repeat the sauce and filling, then cover with a third slice of toast. Make three more sandwiches in the same way.

Secure each sandwich with four toothpicks and cut into four diagonally. Serve the remaining sauce on the side.

Hamming it up

Jambon de Paris, prosciutto, anchovy, tapenade and sun-dried tomato Sandwiches

PREPARATION TIME: 20 MINUTES

MAKES 10

1¼ cups pitted black olives
1 garlic clove
scant 1 cup olive oil
20 slices of white bread, crusts removed
3 slices of jambon de Paris (see page 102) or other unsmoked,
   fully-cooked ham, cut into strips
3 slices of prosciutto, cut into strips
10 sun-dried tomatoes in oil, drained and cut into strips
1 onion, sliced and fried
10 salted anchovies

Put the olives, garlic, and olive oil in a blender and process to make the tapenade.

Toast the bread in a toaster or under a preheated broiler and spread the tapenade on one side of each slice.

Add the strips of jambon de Paris or other unsmoked ham and prosciutto, the sun-dried tomatoes, fried onion, and anchovies to half the slices. Top with the remaining slices of toast.

TAPENADE

Tapenade is a paste made from finely chopped olives, capers and anchovies. The dish comes originally from Provence and is now popular all over the Mediterranean. It is delicious both on its own, on toast, or as part of a more elaborate dish.

Fourme d'Ambert cheese quiche

PREPARATION TIME: 20 MINUTES
COOKING TIME: 30 MINUTES

SERVES 6

3½ ounces fresh pork rind
generous ½ cup fresh pork belly, cut into batons
3 eggs
2¼ cups fresh whole milk
a pinch of freshly grated nutmeg
12 ounces pie dough, thawed if frozen
all-purpose flour, for dusting
3½ ounces sharp Fourme d'Ambert or other hard
  blue cheese, crumbled

Preheat the oven to 350°F. Blanch the rind in a large pan of boiling water until it has softened completely. Blanch the pork belly in another pan of boiling water. Drain both and slice the rind.

Beat the eggs with the milk in a bowl and add the nutmeg. Roll out the dough on a lightly floured surface and use to line a 9-inch quiche pan. Trim the edge, prick the base with a fork, and place on a cookie sheet. Add the crumbled cheese, sliced rind, and pork belly batons.

Pour in the egg and milk mixture and bake in the oven for 30 minutes or until the mixture is just set.

Quiche with two kinds of ham

PREPARATION TIME: 10 MINUTES
COOKING TIME: 30 MINUTES

SERVES 6

4 eggs
⅔ cup heavy cream
2¼ cups fresh whole milk
12 ounces pie dough, thawed if frozen
all-purpose flour, for dusting
1 cup diced jambon de Paris (see page 102)
  or other unsmoked, fully-cooked ham
5 ounces sharp Comté or Gruyère cheese, diced
3 slices of prosciutto or other dry-cured ham,
  cut into thin strips
½ cup shelled walnuts, chopped

Preheat the oven to 350°F. Beat the eggs with the cream and milk in a bowl.

Roll out the dough on a lightly floured surface and use to line a 9-inch quiche pan. Trim the edge, prick the base, and place on a cookie sheet. Add the diced ham, cheese, prosciutto, and walnuts.

Pour in the egg mixture and bake for 30 minutes or until the mixture is just set.

Hamming it up

Croque Monsieur snacks (thanks Véro)

PREPARATION TIME: 15 MINUTES
COOKING TIME: 5 MINUTES

MAKES 12

2¼ cups grated Swiss cheese
scant ½ cup crème fraîche
3 slices of jambon de Paris (see page 102)
  or other unsmoked, fully-cooked ham
6 slices of country-style white bread

It's Sunday evening and the kids are starving: here's the ideal snack for satisfying all appetites with something tasty that can be made in no time.

Preheat the broiler. Combine the Swiss cheese and crème fraîche in a bowl. Divide the ham between 3 slices of bread, cover with some of the cheese mixture, and top with the remaining slices of bread. Spoon over the remaining cheese mixture and broil until golden and bubbling. Cut each sandwich into four pieces before serving.

You can garnish your snacks with chives, onions, or spices, if you like.

Hamming it up

Smoked ham focaccia

PREPARATION AND RISING TIME: 1¼ HOURS
COOKING TIME: 30 MINUTES

MAKES 1 LOAF

¾ ounce fresh yeast
1 cup lukewarm water
3½ cups bread flour
scant ½ cup olive oil
½ teaspoon fine salt
5 ounces smoked ham or Canadian bacon, cut into batons
sea salt and coarsely ground black pepper

Mash the yeast with half the lukewarm water to a paste in a bowl. Sift the flour into another bowl, add the remaining water, the olive oil, yeast, and fine salt, and mix to a springy dough, using a mixer fitted with dough hooks. Add the ham.

Shape the dough into a ball and turn out onto a board covered with waxed paper. Cover with a damp dish towel and let rise at room temperature for about 1 hour, until it has doubled in volume.

Preheat the oven to 475°F. Shape the dough into an oval or round, place it on a cookie sheet, and slash the top with a knife. Sprinkle with sea salt and coarsely ground black pepper. Bake for about 30 minutes, checking frequently toward the end of the cooking time.

Hamming it up

Vegetable and basil tart with prosciutto

PREPARATION TIME: 30 MINUTES
COOKING TIME: 30 MINUTES

SERVES 6

7 tablespoons olive oil, plus extra for drizzling
2 onions, sliced
1 eggplant, sliced
2 zucchini, sliced
12 ounces puff pastry dough, thawed if frozen
all-purpose flour, for dusting
6–8 cherry tomatoes
4 slices of dry-cured ham such as prosciutto
  or Toulouse ham, cut into strips
1 bunch of fresh basil
sea salt

Preheat the oven to 325°F. Heat 3 tablespoons of the olive oil in a skillet. Add the onions and cook over very low heat, stirring occasionally, for 10–15 minutes, until very soft but not colored. Meanwhile, heat 3 tablespoons of the remaining olive oil in another pan. Add the eggplant and zucchini and cook, stirring occasionally, for about 5 minutes, until tender crisp.

Roll out the dough to a round on a lightly floured surface, then transfer to a cookie sheet. Cover the dough round with the softened onions and place the eggplant and zucchini on top. Add the cherry tomatoes and strips of ham. Drizzle with olive oil and sprinkle with sea salt. Bake in the oven for 30 minutes.

Toward the end of the cooking time, heat the remaining olive oil in a small skillet. Add the basil leaves and fry for a few minutes. Remove with a slotted spoon, sprinkle them over the tart, and serve immediately.

Hamming it up

The pig goes east

THE PIG GOES EAST

EXPORTED, IMPORTED, THE PIG IS INTERNATIONAL!

Pigs from the East turn up in many different forms to please our Western palates. Eastern pork products are rich in spicy flavors and include sweet – sour varieties.

Trust the gastronomic wealth offered by the Asiatic pig and let some unlikely flavor combinations surprise you. No pig ever looks very unhappy on the Great Wall of China. And pigs are a lot of fun in the Land of the Rising Sun.

✳

Steamed pork buns

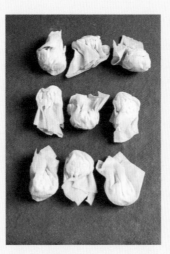

Pork wontons

Steamed pork puffs

Citronella sausages

Pork dim sum

Cooked pig's blood

Thai pork pâté

Pig's tripe

Sausage with
black mushrooms

Pâtés and terrines

Roast pork with thyme and parsley

PREPARATION TIME: 30 MINUTES
COOKING TIME: 2 HOURS

SERVES 6

1 boneless fresh picnic ham
1 pork tenderloin
3 fresh thyme sprigs
1 bunch of fresh parsley, finely chopped
5 garlic cloves, finely chopped
2 shallots, finely chopped
salt and coarsely ground black pepper

Preheat the oven to 325°F. Trim the picnic ham, then cut it into a rectangle the same length as the tenderloin. Remove the leaves from the thyme and mix with the parsley. Sprinkle the mixture over the picnic ham, then sprinkle with the garlic and shallots. Season well with salt.

Place the tenderloin along one side of the picnic ham, then roll up the pork tightly. Tie with kitchen string and roll in pepper.

Roast in the oven, turning frequently, for 2 hours, until highly caramelized. The roast can be eaten hot or cold.

René

LIKE MY GRANDPA BUT WITH MORE HAIR

René, now the head of the Barbe butcher's store, is Grandpa's worthy successor. For many years he had to compromise between Grandpa, with his firm ideas of how it ought to be run, and his own sensible way of adapting to new regulations. He patiently used his expertise to make the Barbe shop into a really high-class establishment. Although he has been retired for five years now, not an extra ounce of weight spoils the fit of his professional clothing, a uniform which may be short on gold braid but is worn with passionate commitment.

*

René's pâté

PREPARATION TIME: 30 MINUTES
COOKING TIME: 1½ HOURS
STANDING TIME: 48 HOURS

MAKES 2¼ POUNDS

2 pounds boneless fatty pork, from the shoulder
¼ pound fresh pork belly
4 garlic cloves, chopped
3 shallots, chopped
scant ½ cup white wine
¼ cup rum
scant ½ cup heavy cream
2 eggs, lightly beaten
1 teaspoon Quatre-épices (see below)
3 ounces thinly sliced fresh pork fat or 6–8 slices
  of bacon, blanched
2 bay leaves
2 fresh thyme sprigs
salt and pepper

Preheat the oven to 350°F. Grind all the meat except the fat with the coarse blade of a meat grinder or in a food processor and place in a bowl. Add the garlic, shallots, wine, rum, cream, eggs, and spice, season with salt and pepper, and mix well until thoroughly combined.

Line a terrine with some of the fat, fill with the prepared mixture, smooth the top, and cover with the remaining fat. Place the bay leaves on top and sprinkle with the thyme leaves. Cover with the lid and place in a roasting pan. Pour enough boiling water into the pan to come about halfway up the sides of the terrine and bake in the oven for 1½ hours.

Let the terrine stand for 48 hours before serving.

QUATRE-ÉPICES

Quatre-épices usually includes four or five spices, but here's a blend that includes all five. The recipe is a suggestion only: these proportions are typical but the spice blend can be varied to suit one's own palate. Put all of the following in a spice mill or blender and process until evenly ground. Store in a cool, dark place: 2 tablespoons (⅛ cup) white peppercorns, ¼ teaspoon freshly grated nutmeg; ½ teaspoon (about 12) whole cloves; ¼ teaspoon cinnamon; ¼ teaspoon ground ginger.

Terrine beaujolais

PREPARATION TIME: 30 MINUTES
STANDING TIME: 3 HOURS, PLUS 48 HOURS
COOKING TIME: 2 HOURS

MAKES 3¼ POUNDS

1 pounds 2 ounces pig's liver
3 ounces smoked bacon
4½ ounces pork fat
1¼ pounds boneless fatty pork, cut from the shoulder
6 garlic cloves, chopped
2 onions, chopped
2¼ cups Beaujolais wine
¼ cup cognac or brandy
1 teaspoon freshly grated nutmeg
3½ ounces pig's caul fat, to be ordered from your
   butcher (see *Sources*)
salt and pepper

Grind all the meat with the coarse blade of a meat grinder or in a food processor and place in a bowl. Add the garlic, onions, wine, cognac or brandy, and nutmeg, season with salt and pepper, and mix well until thoroughly combined.

Fill a terrine with this mixture and cover with the caul fat. Let stand in the refrigerator for 3 hours. Preheat the oven to 350°F.

Place the terrine in a roasting pan. Add boiling water to the pan, to come about halfway up the sides of the terrine. Bake for 2 hours, until the top is well browned.

Let the terrine stand for 48 hours before serving.

Bibi

BISTRO OWNER OF THE NEW GENERATION

A bistro manager of the new generation, his paunch as welcoming as a soft pillow to a tired head at night, Bibi has such a tuneful accent that you need a musical ear to decode everything he says.

He wears a shirt so freshly ironed that when he starts serving guests it almost smells like the flowers of the field; by the time he's finished serving it has begun to look like a field full of flowers.

Resembling the singers Dany Brillant and Dario Moreno, Bibi had the looks for a career in show business himself, but he went in for bistro management the way other men might kiss a pretty girl – with passion and pride and that little extra something which brings customers back to his place.

✳

Bibi's head-to-foot terrine

PREPARATION TIME: 45 MINUTES
COOKING TIME: 3 HOURS 20 MINUTES
STANDING TIME: 24 HOURS

MAKES 3¼ POUNDS

4 pig's feet
4 pig's cheeks (meat only), to be ordered from your
    butcher (see *Sources*)
2 pig's snouts
3 pig's ears
2 pig's tongues
1 pound boneless fatty pork, cut from the shoulder
4 onions
4 cloves
6 carrots
2 leeks, halved
1 celery root, cut into chunks
1 fennel bulb, cut into fourths
2 bay leaves
4 garlic cloves
salt and pepper

Put all the meat in a large pan. Stud the onions with the cloves and add to the pan with the carrots, leeks, celery root, fennel, bay leaves, and garlic. Pour in water to cover and bring to a boil, then lower the heat, and simmer for 3 hours.

Remove the meat from the pan with a slotted spoon and reserve the stock. Cut the meat off the bones. Coarsely chop all the meat, place in a bowl, mix well, and season with salt and pepper.

Return the pan of stock to a boil, without removing the vegetables, and cook until reduced to 4 cups. Strain into a clean bowl and discard the vegetables and flavorings.

Place the meat in a terrine, cover with the reduced stock, and let set in a cold place for 24 hours.

Easter ham (or parsley ham)

PREPARATION TIME: 20 MINUTES
SOAKING TIME: 24 HOURS
COOKING TIME: 3½ HOURS
STANDING TIME: 48 HOURS

SERVES 10

4½ pounds slightly salted ham
  (see page 214 for brining instructions)
2 onions
6 cloves
4 pig's feet
4 carrots
2 leeks
2 celery stalks
7 ounces fresh parsley, leaves finely chopped and stalks reserved
2 fresh thyme sprigs
2 bay leaves
6¼ cups Burgundy or Chardonnay wine
6 shallots, finely chopped
1 garlic bulb, finely chopped
coarsely ground black pepper

Soak the ham in cold water for 24 hours to remove the salt, changing the water several times. (This step is not necessary if you have brined the meat yourself.)

Drain the ham, place in a large flameproof casserole, add water to cover, and bring to a boil. Lower the heat and simmer for 45 minutes, then drain, and rinse. Meanwhile, stud the onions with the cloves. Return the ham to the casserole and add the pig's feet, carrots, leeks, celery, parsley stalks, onions, thyme, bay leaves, and wine, and season with pepper. Add sufficient water to cover the ham and bring to a boil. Lower the heat, cover, and simmer for 2½ hours, until the ham is very tender.

Remove the ham from the casserole and cut it into large cubes. Bring the stock back to a boil and reduce to 4 cups, then strain, and let cool. Combine the chopped parsley leaves, shallots, and garlic in a bowl. Make alternate layers of diced ham and the parsley mixture in a terrine. If you like, you can also dice the carrots used for cooking the ham and include them. Pour in the cooled stock.

Cover and let set in the refrigerator for 48 hours. You can serve the Easter ham with a shallot-mustard vinaigrette as dressing.

A specialty from Burgundy, this terrine is traditionally eaten at Easter, the period when hams are taken out of the salting rooms.

pig's head and parsley pâté

PREPARATION TIME: 1 HOUR
COOKING TIME: 4½ HOURS
STANDING TIME: 24 HOURS

MAKES 2¼ POUNDS

2 onions
4 cloves
½ pig's head with tongue
11 ounces Boston butt
2 pig's feet
2 turnips
2 carrots
2 leeks
3 bay leaves
1 bunch of fresh parsley, finely chopped
2 shallots, finely chopped
salt and pepper

Stud the onions with the cloves. Put the pig's head, Boston butt, feet, clove-studded onions, turnips, carrots, leeks, and bay leaves in a large flameproof casserole. Add water to cover and bring to a boil. Cook for 4 hours.

Remove all the meat from the casserole with a slotted spoon. Cut the meat from the bones and mix together in a bowl. Remove the carrots and leeks from the casserole with a slotted spoon, dice, and add to the meat. Season with salt and pepper and stir in the parsley and shallots.

Strain the stock into a clean pan and bring to a boil, then cook until well reduced. Remove from the heat and let cool.

Pile the meat mixture into a terrine, cover with cooled stock, and let set in the refrigerator for at least 24 hours.

SOME BACKGROUND

Pig's head pâté is generally prepared with all the leftover meat from the slaughtered pig. The carcass is taken away and cooked for several hours in a beef stock with the feet and head. The meat is then removed from the bones, mixed with a persillade – parsley and garlic mixture – then placed in a terrine, and covered with reduced stock.

Warm pâté

PREPARATION TIME: 45 MINUTES
COOKING TIME: 45 MINUTES

SERVES 6

14 ounces jambon de Paris (see page 102)
  or other unsmoked, fully-cooked ham, finely chopped
2 shallots, finely chopped
1 garlic clove, finely chopped
11 ounces bulk (breakfast) sausage
generous ½ cup chopped smoked bacon
scant ½ cup heavy cream
3 egg yolks
¼ cup port
a pinch of ground ginger
a pinch of curry powder
a pinch of Quatre-épices (see page 154)
12 ounces pie dough, thawed if frozen
all-purpose flour, for dusting
12 ounces puff pastry dough, thawed if frozen

FOR THE SAUCE

3 tablespoons sweet butter
4 shallots, chopped
scant ½ cup white port
1¼ cups heavy cream

Preheat the oven to 325°F. Combine the ham, shallots, garlic, bulk sausage, and chopped bacon in a bowl. Add the cream, 2 of the egg yolks, the port, and the spices.

Roll out the pie dough on a lightly floured surface and use to line a deep pie dish or terrine, leaving an overhang at the sides. Roll out the puff pastry dough on a lightly floured surface. Fill the pie dish with the ham mixture, lightly beat the remaining egg yolk, and brush the overhanging pie dough with some of it. Cover with the puff pastry dough and seal by pinching the sides together. Cut an opening in the top and insert a funnel of wax or parchment paper to let steam escape during cooking. Brush the top with the remaining egg yolk and bake in the oven for 45 minutes.

Meanwhile, to prepare the sauce, melt the butter in a small pan. Add the shallots and cook over low heat, stirring occasionally, for about 8 minutes, until softened and lightly colored. Stir in the white port and cook until reduced. Stir in the cream and heat through gently but do not let it boil. Serve the pâté warm, coated with the shallot cream.

Parfait of pig's liver and Muscatel

PREPARATION TIME: 20 MINUTES
COOKING TIME: 10 MINUTES

MAKES 10 × 3½-oz POTS

1 pound 2 ounces pig's liver, diced
generous ½ cup chopped smoked bacon
3 shallots, finely chopped
2 garlic cloves, finely chopped
12 juniper berries, crushed
1 teaspoon sugar
4 teaspoons brandy
2½ cups Muscatel, white port or Sauternes wine
1⅓ cups slightly salted butter
¼ cup heavy cream
1 envelope granulated gelatin
salt and pepper

Cook the liver, bacon, shallots, garlic, and juniper berries in a pan over medium heat, stirring frequently, for about 5 minutes, until evenly browned. Stir in the sugar, add the brandy, and ignite. When the flames have died down, add half the wine and cook, scraping up any sediment from the base of the pan with a wooden spoon, until reduced to a syrup. Remove the pan from the heat and stir in the butter and cream. Season with salt and pepper.

Spoon the mixture into ten ramekins or other small pots, filling them no more than two-thirds full, and let cool.

Place the gelatin in a small bowl of water, stir and let stand for 5 minutes. Meanwhile, heat the remaining wine in a pan. Remove the pan from the heat and add the gelatin. Let cool to room temperature, then pour a layer of gelatin over the parfaits, and place in the refrigerator to set.

Remove the parfaits from the refrigerator 20–30 minutes before serving with toasted rustic bread.

Pâtés and terrines

Plain and simple rillons

MARINATING TIME: 24 HOURS
PREPARATION TIME: 15 MINUTES
COOKING TIME: 2¼ HOURS

SERVES 4

2¼ pounds fresh pork belly
1½ tablespoons salt
1 teaspoon Quatre-épices (see page 154)
2 cups fresh lard
3 tablespoons sugar

Cut the meat into 2-inch cubes. Place them in a bowl, add the salt and spice, mix well, and let marinate in the refrigerator for 24 hours.

Melt the lard in a large pan. Add the pork and cook over medium heat, stirring frequently, for about 10 minutes, until lightly browned all over. Lower the heat and simmer gently for about 2 hours, until tender. Stir in the sugar and cook, stirring frequently, until the meat is caramelized.

The rillons can be eaten hot or cold.

RILLONS

Rillons are pieces of pork belly that have been cooked slowly in fat (caramelized) in a covered pot. They are often served at breakfast, or as a side dish or with fruit.

Lyonnais pork cracklings

BOUGHT FROM ANY GOOD PORK BUTCHER

If you're out in the Halle de Lyon food market with your fiancée, make sure you're clever enough to be invited to taste something. And make sure you're not ripped off when you take out your wallet. Don't be reluctant to pour a glass of freshly drawn Beaujolais down your throat either. 'No drinking without something to eat' – that's the motto of the people of Lyon. So treat yourself to a plate of pork snacks the size of walnuts. You'll be licking your lips and all five fingers ... and there's no risk of indigestion as they provide good healthy food in Lyon!

*

Pâtés and terrines

Pork rillettes

PREPARATION TIME: 15 MINUTES
COOKING TIME: 4 HOURS

MAKES 6 × 9-oz POTS

11 ounces fresh pork fat or lard
2¼ cups dry white wine
2 onions, sliced
1 fresh rosemary sprig
1 bay leaf
2¼ pounds boneless fatty pork from the shoulder, diced
7 ounces smoked slab bacon, diced
salt and pepper

Put the fat, white wine, onions, rosemary, and bay leaf in a pan and heat gently until the fat has melted. Add the meat and cook over very low heat, stirring frequently, for 3–4 hours, until the meat breaks up.

Using a slotted spoon, transfer the meat to a bowl and discard the herbs. Season the meat with salt and pepper and spoon it into six 9-oz pots, pressing it down well. Spoon some of the melted fat over the top of each pot to cover and let cool.

RILLETTES

Essentially potted meat, rillettes is pork meat that has been slowly cooked in fat, shredded and pounded to a smooth paste, then mixed with enough of the cooking fat to form a paste. After cooking, the mixture is packed into a terrine or ramekin and allowed to cool. Rillettes are most commonly spread on bread or toast.

Pork confit

PREPARATION TIME: 20 MINUTES
MARINATING TIME: 24 HOURS
COOKING TIME: 2 HOURS

MAKES 4 × 1-lb-2-oz POTS

1¼ pounds boneless fatty pork from the shoulder
1¼ pounds fresh pork belly
1¼ cups sugar
a pinch of salt
1 teaspoon paprika
1 teaspoon dried thyme
1 bay leaf, crumbled
2¼ pounds duck fat
1 pound 2 ounces fresh pork fat or lard

Cut the fatty pork and belly each into four pieces and place on a large plate. Combine the sugar, salt, paprika, thyme, and bay leaf in a bowl, then sprinkle the mixture all over the meat. Cover and let marinate in the refrigerator for 24 hours.

Wipe all the pieces of meat with damp paper towels. Melt the duck fat and pork fat or lard in a pan over very low heat. Add the meat and cook gently for 2 hours, until very tender and easily pierced with a needle.

Pour a layer of fat into each of four 1-pound-2-ounce pots and let set. Gently lay a slice of the pork and a piece of belly on top of each, then cover completely with fat. Let set.

CONFIT

Confit is one of the oldest ways to preserve food. It describes food that has been cooked in its own juices, to both flavor and preserve it. Sealed and stored in a cool place, confit can last for several months.

Pork confit tart

PREPARATION TIME: 45 MINUTES
COOKING TIME: 45 MINUTES

SERVES 8

2 tablespoons olive oil
2 onions, sliced
1 pound 2 ounces pork confit (see page 176),
   coarsely chopped
1 bunch of fresh basil, finely chopped
1 bunch of fresh chives, finely chopped
6 large potatoes, cut into thin rounds
scant 1 cup crème fraîche
1 teaspoon ground cumin
1 pound puff pastry dough, thawed if frozen
all-purpose flour, for dusting
1 egg yolk, lightly beaten
salt and pepper

Heat the olive oil in a large pan. Add the onions and cook over low heat, stirring occasionally, for 5 minutes, until softened but not colored. Add the confit, basil, and chives and mix well.

Meanwhile, blanch the potatoes in boiling water for a few minutes, then drain, and cool. Process the onion and confit mixture in a food processor until finely ground. Mix the cooled potato rounds with the crème fraîche and cumin in a bowl and season with salt and pepper. Preheat the oven to 325°F.

Cut the pastry dough into two pieces, one slightly larger than the other. Roll out the larger piece on a lightly floured surface and use to line a pie dish. Spoon in the ground confit and cover with the potato mixture. Brush the rim of the pie with some of the beaten egg yolk. Roll out the remaining pastry dough and use to cover the pie, pressing the edges together to seal. Brush the top with the remaining egg yolk and cut a slit to let the steam escape during cooking. Place on a cookie sheet and bake in the oven for 45 minutes.

La Caillette

PREPARATION TIME: 1 HOUR
COOKING TIME: 1¾ HOURS

MAKES 20 SMALL SAUSAGES

1 cabbage, shredded
2¼ pounds boneless picnic ham,
  ground or finely chopped
1 pound 2 ounces pig's liver,
  ground or finely chopped
11 ounces fresh pork belly or unsmoked bacon,
  ground or finely chopped
7 ounces smoked bacon, ground or finely chopped
2 shallots, chopped
1 bunch of fresh parsley, chopped
5 garlic cloves, chopped
2 eggs
scant ½ cup port
pork caul fat (ordered from your butcher),
  soaked to soften
about ½ bottle (1⅔ cups) dry white wine
salt and pepper

Preheat the oven to 325°F. Cook the cabbage in boiling water until tender, then drain, and dry by rolling it in a dish towel. Place all the meat in a bowl and season with salt and pepper. Add the shallots, parsley, garlic, eggs, port, and cabbage and mix well until thoroughly combined.

Divide the mixture into 20 portions, each weighing about 3½ ounces (you can make them smaller if they are to be served as appetizers). Wrap each portion in caul fat and place in a single layer in an ovenproof dish in which they fit snugly. Pour in white wine to reach as far as the top. Bake in the oven for 1½ hours.

The caillettes may be eaten hot or cold.

PREPARATION TIME: 1 HOUR
COOKING TIME: 1¾ HOURS

MAKES 20 SMALL SAUSAGES

1¾ pounds chard
olive oil
2 garlic cloves, crushed
2¼ pounds boneless picnic ham,
  ground or finely chopped
1 pounds 2 ounces pig's liver, ground
  or finely chopped
1 pound 2 ounces fresh pork belly or unsmoked
  bacon, ground or finely chopped
2 shallots, chopped
1 bunch of fresh parsley, chopped
5 garlic cloves, chopped
2 eggs
scant ½ cup port
pork caul fat (ordered from your butcher),
  soaked to soften
about ½ bottle (1⅔ cups) dry white wine
salt and pepper

In this version, the cabbage is replaced with chard, considered to be more digestible. Cut out the stems from the chard and slice them very thinly. Blanch the stems in salted boiling water for 10–15 minutes, then drain. Blanch the green leaves in salted boiling water for about 5 minutes, then drain, and chop. Heat the olive oil in a skillet. Add the chard stems and crushed garlic and cook over low heat, stirring occasionally, for about 5 minutes.

Finish making the cailettes as in the recipe on the left.

Pâtés and terrines

Marcou and Paulette

PURE POETRY

Grandpa Barbe's sausages were pure poetry for Marcou and Paulette, especially his caillettes. Representatives of the old rural tradition and loyal suppliers to Grandpa Barbe, Marcou and Paulette kept his store stocked with pork, veal, beef, and mutton for years.

An expert on caillettes, Marcou thought Grandpa's were perfection. If you hear him singing their praises, you'll feel an irresistible urge to sit down and satisfy your appetite for those delicious pork and herb sausages. Even Pavlov would find it hard to compete with Marcou when he's on form!

✳

Pig's tongue with sorrel

PREPARATION TIME: 30 MINUTES
COOKING TIME: 45 MINUTES

SERVES 6

6 pig's tongues
2 onions
2 carrots
1 leek
1¾ pounds small potatoes, halved
3 slices of smoked slab bacon, about ½ inch thick
2 shallots, chopped
1 small jar of sorrel preserve
¾ cup Muscatel, white port or Sauternes wine
scant 1 cup heavy cream

Put the tongues in a large pan, pour in water to cover, and add the onions, carrots, and leek. Bring to a boil, then lower the heat, and simmer for 45 minutes. Meanwhile, parboil the potatoes in water for about 10 minutes, then drain. Cut the bacon into large batons. Put the batons, shallots, and potatoes in a skillet and cook over medium–low heat, stirring frequently, until they are well browned and the potatoes are tender.

Heat the sorrel preserve with the wine in a pan. Add the cream and cook until slightly reduced.

Drain the tongues and remove and discard the first layer of skin. Slice the meat.

Place a reassembled sliced tongue on each serving plate and pour the sorrel sauce over it. Serve with the potatoes.

SORREL PRESERVE

Sorrel preserve may be available from French delicatessens. If you cannot find it, use 1 pound 2 ounces fresh sorrel (or spinach). Shred it finely and sauté in 5 tablespoons sweet butter in a half-covered pan over very low heat until all traces of liquid have gone. Then proceed as in the recipe above.

Baby spinach and pig's ear salad

PREPARATION TIME: 30 MINUTES
COOKING TIME: 1¼ HOURS

SERVES 6

3 pig's ears
2 shallots, finely chopped
1-inch piece of fresh ginger root, finely chopped
1 bunch of fresh chives, chopped
scant ½ cup canola oil
oil, for frying
1 tablespoon raspberry vinegar
14 ounces baby spinach

Cook the pig's ears in a large pan of boiling water for 1 hour, then drain and let cool. Combine the shallots, ginger, chives, and canola oil.

Once the pig's ears have cooled, thinly slice them. Heat the oil for frying in a skillet, add the meat, and cook over high heat, stirring frequently, for a few minutes, until evenly browned. Stir in the raspberry vinegar, scraping up any sediment from the base of the skillet with a wooden spoon.

Combine the spinach with the shallot mixture and pile into a dome on individual serving plates. Sprinkle with the fried pig's ears and serve.

Stuffed pig's ears

PREPARATION TIME: 20 MINUTES
COOKING TIME: 3 HOURS

SERVES 6

1 onion
2 cloves
3 carrots
1 leek
3 pig's feet
3 pig's ears
3½ ounces sweetbreads
1 zucchini, diced
2 tomatoes, peeled and diced
2 ounces foie gras, diced
1 shallot, finely chopped
3 fresh chives, finely chopped
3 fresh tarragon sprigs, finely chopped
salt and pepper

FOR THE SAUCE

1 egg
2½ cups olive oil
1 teaspoon balsamic vinegar
1 tablespoon Meaux or other grain mustard

Stud the onion with the cloves and place in a large pan with the carrots, leek, and feet. Add water to cover and bring to a boil, then lower the heat, and cook for 2 hours. Add the pig's ears and simmer for a further 30 minutes. Add the sweetbreads and simmer for 30 minutes more.

Remove the pan from the heat and lift out the feet with a slotted spoon. Cut off the meat and discard the bones. Remove the ears with a slotted spoon. Thinly slice one ear. Lift out the sweetbreads and carrots and dice both. Set the whole ears aside and mix the remaining meat, sweetbreads, and carrots together.

Blanch the zucchini in boiling water for 1–2 minutes, then drain, and add to the meat mixture with the tomatoes, foie gras, shallot, chives, and tarragon. Mix well and season with salt and pepper.

Spoon the mixture into one of the warm ears and cover with the other ear, placed the opposite way round. Roll firmly in plastic wrap and let stand in a cool place to set.

Meanwhile, make the sauce. Whisk the egg with a pinch of salt, then gradually whisk in the olive oil, 1–2 teaspoons at a time, until one fourth has been added. Whisk in the balsamic vinegar, then continue whisking in the oil, adding it in a thin, steady stream. Whisk in the mustard.

Unwrap the stuffed ears and cut into thin slices, then serve with the mustard mayonnaise.

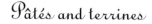

Pig's feet with walnut oil and caramelized onion

PREPARATION TIME: 30 MINUTES
COOKING TIME: 3¼ HOURS

SERVES 6

10 pig's feet
7 ounces smoked slab bacon
5 brown onions
3 carrots
1 leek
1 bunch of fresh parsley
3 bay leaves
1 cup walnut oil
1 teaspoon brown sugar
1 tablespoon balsamic vinegar
1 red onion, sliced
1 bunch of fresh chives, chopped
sea salt
coarsely ground black pepper

Put the feet, bacon, 2 of the brown onions, the carrots, leek, parsley, and bay leaves in a large pan, add water to cover, and bring to a boil. Lower the heat and simmer for 3 hours.

Chop 2 of the remaining brown onions. Heat scant ½ cup of the walnut oil in a skillet, add the chopped onions, and cook over very low heat, stirring occasionally, for 10 minutes, until very soft but not colored.

Remove the feet and bacon from the pan with a slotted spoon. Cut the meat from the feet and chop it finely. Chop the bacon. Stir the meat and bacon into the softened onions and season with salt and pepper. Shape the mixture into sausage shapes, 1¼ inches in diameter, and wrap in plastic wrap. Let stand in a cool place to set.

Slice the remaining brown onion. Heat scant ½ cup of the remaining oil in a skillet, add the sliced onion, and cook over high heat, stirring frequently, for 10 minutes, until softened and golden brown. Stir in the brown sugar and cook, stirring, until the onion has caramelized.

Whisk together the rest of the remaining oil and the balsamic vinegar in a bowl and season with salt and pepper. Preheat the broiler.

Unwrap the sausage shapes and cut into ¼-inch-thick slices. Arrange them on a flameproof dish and cook briefly under the broiler until hot. Season with sea salt and coarsely ground black pepper and sprinkle with the vinaigrette. Add the caramelized onion, red onion, and chives and serve.

Crunchy crépinettes with nuts

PREPARATION TIME: 20 MINUTES
COOKING TIME: 3½ HOURS

SERVES 6

6 pig's feet
3 pig's ears
3½ ounces fresh pork belly
6 tablespoons olive oil
3 garlic cloves, coarsely chopped
14 ounces spinach, coarse stalks removed
grated rind of 1 lemon
¼ cup coarsely chopped peanuts
7 ounces caul fat (see *Sources*), soaked to soften
1 onion, grated
6 large potatoes, grated
1 shallot, finely chopped
2 eggs
1 bunch of fresh chives, chopped
⅔ cup crème fraîche

Put the feet, ears, and fresh pork belly in a large pan, add water to cover, and bring to a boil. Lower the heat and cook for 3 hours, then drain. Cut the meat from the feet and chop it coarsely with the ears and belly. Heat 3 tablespoons of the oil in a large pan. Add the garlic and cook over low heat, stirring occasionally, until it is just beginning to color. Add the spinach, lemon rind, peanuts, and meat and cook, stirring occasionally, until the mixture has softened and collapsed. Form the mixture into six balls and wrap them in the caul fat. Store the crépinettes the refrigerator until required – you can leave them for several days if you wish.

Combine the onion, potato, shallot, eggs and half the chives in a bowl. Heat 2 tablespoons of the remaining oil in a skillet and add the onion and potato mixture, pressing it down with a spatula. Cook the galette until it is golden brown on the underside, then turn it over, and cook until the second side is golden brown. (The easiest way to turn it is to place a plate over the pan and invert the two, then slide the galette back into the skillet with the cooked side uppermost.) You can cook a large galette and cut it into triangles or six individual galettes. Preheat the oven to 350°F.

Mix the crème fraîche with the remaining oil and chives. Heat a skillet that can be transferred to the oven. Add the crépinettes and cook, turning occasionally, until browned. Transfer to the oven and cook for a further for 10 minutes. Place a triangle of the large galette or a small galette on each of six serving plates. Put a crépinette on top and spoon the chive cream over it. Serve immediately.

The genuine Charcutier's Meatloaf

PREPARATION TIME: 30 MINUTES
COOKING TIME: 45 MINUTES

MAKES 1 LOAF

sweet butter, for greasing
2¼ cups all-purpose flour, plus extra for dusting
4 tablespoons olive oil
3 shallots, chopped
1½ teaspoons baking powder
4 eggs, lightly beaten
scant ½ cup white wine
scant 1 cup fresh whole milk
generous ½ cup coarsely chopped smoked bacon
generous ½ cup coarsely chopped jambon de Paris
  (see page 102) or other unsmoked, fully-cooked ham
scant ¼ cup coarsely chopped spicy Spanish chorizo
  sausage (see pages 68 and 69) or Mexican chorizo
  (see *Sources*) cooked, drained and cut into small pieces
generous ½ cup coarsely chopped prosciutto

Preheat the oven to 325°F. Grease a loaf pan with butter and dust with flour, tipping out any excess.

Heat 2 tablespoons of the olive oil in a skillet. Add the shallots and cook over low heat, stirring occasionally, for about 10 minutes, until golden brown.

Sift the flour and baking powder into a bowl, add the eggs, white wine, milk, and remaining olive oil and mix well. Stir in all the meat and the shallots. Pour the mixture into the prepared pan and bake in the oven for 45 minutes.

CHARCUTERIE

The term charcuterie is used to describe both the branch of cooking devoted to cooked or processed meat products, primarily from pork, and a shop selling these products. A charcutier is the man or woman behind the counter, and they are usually a great source of information and advice on pork.

January,

somewhere in Les Landes,

the Pâté Team

Pompon

Stéphane

SO HOW DO YOU GET
A PÂTÉ TEAM TOGETHER?

First you need to be in luck and find the right people at the right time. In my own case, several pints of Guinness in an Irish-style pub on the eve of a Five Nations rugby match (and writing that doesn't make me feel any younger), a cigar smoked (with some difficulty) in the Palais des Congrès on the day of the match itself, and a number of songs after the match, once again in an Irish-style pub, were a real revelation about friendship and sincerity. We would find out more about each other in the future, but it was obvious that we weren't going to split up.

Getting a good pâté-making team together calls for careful selection of the members. First you need a Jacquy, the indispensable team coach. He is the brains of the whole thing, the real boss. It is true that it's not easy to find someone like him today, but if you search the bars of Épernon carefully, you might find one. If you do, then take my advice and hang on to him. A man like Jacquy is a precious find!

And once you have a Jacquy you need a Pompon, the other star of the world of pâté. Pompon is the backbone of the organization, a veritable walking encyclopedia on the history and origin of all good pâtés. You also need the gentle touch added to the team, in our case in the form of Kiki Pompon and Catie ... but beware, that gentle touch is only on the surface and can sometimes blaze up. (If the pâté dishes of Les Landes can't stand the heat, they should keep out of the kitchen.)

Kiki
Pompon

If, like me, you have the luck to bring such a team together and get to know its members, you'll have many pleasures in store and will wait impatiently, like a child in front of the Christmas tree, for new pâtés to be invented. And if you just can't wait, try something else like diving with dolphins, or psychothermia (no, I'm not sure what that is either) – something with less piggy fun about it, but interesting all the same.

* _jacquy_

Jacquy

THE BACKBONE OF THE WHOLE THING

The backbone of the whole thing, heir to an ancestral pâté recipe, a fine organizer of happy afternoons devoted to charcuterie, Jacquy can't be caught out on the subject of the sausage. He has his own little customs and is famous for them. For instance, he cooks straight lengths of sausage laid out over a bundle of vine shoots which he always lights with the sports page of the newspaper. It seems that in the swirling smoke you can dream of wearing the blue shirt adorned with the French cockerel and of starring on a British rugby field. They say that in Podensac in the Gironde, some people apparently took it into their heads to cook rounds of sausage, and light the fire with another newspaper, just to provoke Jacquy. I suspect some malicious character bearing an old rugby-based grudge of being behind this doctrinal schism over the correct way to cook sausages. (The prime suspect is Bernard, but I say no more. We are making our enquiries.)

Be that as it may, thanks to Jacquy the tradition still goes on. Sausages are cooked as he likes them, we have more and more pâté afternoons, and the distillers of Armagnac brandy needn't shut down just yet.

+ Catie

JACQUY'S WONDERFUL WIFE

She keeps an eye on the quantities and seasoning, she checks anything that goes too far, she tastes the mixture, and gives the go-ahead to the whole recipe.

Pompon

LEARNED PROFESSOR OF PÂTÉ, WELL KNOWN IN THE SAUTERNES AREA

Disciple of Jacquy, chameleon of the digestif

As a keen collector of fine wines and spirits, Pompon is our official Armagnac supplier. Pâté would be a wretched thing without Armagnac — and so would Pompon.

He is the festive spirit behind at least half a dozen pâtés, moderate in everything, and never puts a foot wrong when it comes to celebrating an afternoon of fine charcuterie.

Kiki pompon

POMPON'S WONDERFUL WIFE

She provides the allspice and the meat mixture for the pâté, she's in charge of the evening celebrations, she can dance the fandango, and lead the ensemble ... Kiki Pompon need not blush over her spices, although the spicy pâté itself may color up.

*

jacquy's terrine *

PREPARATION TIME: 1 DAY OR MORE (IT ALL DEPENDS ON HOW MUCH YOUR FRIENDS HELP)
COOKING TIME: 3 HOURS (A FEW ROUNDS OF DRINKS)

MAKES 15 × ½-PINT JARS

5½ pounds fresh pork belly with rind
1¼ pounds pig's liver
Jacquy (it's a good idea to have him around to make the pâté)
4 onions
8 garlic cloves
3 eggs
1 tablespoon piment d'Espelette (see *Sources*), hot paprika,
   or New Mexico chile powder
2 tablespoons salt
1 tablespoon pepper
Pompon (where Jacquy goes, Pompon goes too,
   or the other way round – I can't remember!)
scant ½ cup Armagnac (be generous to allow for tasting!)

Dice the pork belly and liver into large cubes and then grind them with a meat grinder or in a food processor. Have a drink to ward off cramp. Peel and chop the onions. Peel the garlic and remove the green shoots. Have a break and a snack to ward off any cravings. Mix the meat with the eggs, onions, garlic, and piment d'Espelette in a bowl and season with salt and pepper. Sterilize the jars and lids. Ask Pompon to rinse them with the Armagnac, watching him like a hawk. Finish off the Armagnac (if there's any left).

Fill all the jars, making sure that the mixture is pressed down well. Have a walk, have a breather, take a deep breath...

Seal the jars, then place them in a sterilizer or a large pan, and cover them with a weight. Add enough water to reach the top of the pan and bring to a boil. Lower the heat and simmer for 3 hours, checking the level of the water occasionally to make sure that the jars are submerged.

Meanwhile, sample last season's pâtés and plan the date for the next production. Careful, as Jacquy is often unavailable!

It is better to wait a few months before eating the pâté.

* See the following pages for fuller details.

1 Dice the pork belly and the liver into large cubes and grind them both. Have a drink to ward off cramp.

2 Peel and chop the onions. Peel the garlic and remove the shoots. Have a break and a snack to ward off any cravings.

jacquy's
terrine

3 Mix the meat with the eggs, onions, garlic, and piment d'Espelette in a bowl and season with salt and pepper. Sterilize the jars and lids. Ask Pompon to rinse the jars with the Armagnac, watching him like a hawk. Finish off the Armagnac (if there's any left).

4 Fill all the jars, making sure that the mixture is pressed down well. Have a walk, have a breather, take a deep breath . . .

5 Seal the jars, then place them in a sterilizer or a large pan and cover them with a weight. Add enough water to reach the top of the pan and bring to a boil. Lower the heat and simmer for 3 hours, checking the level of the water occasionally to make sure that the jars are submerged.

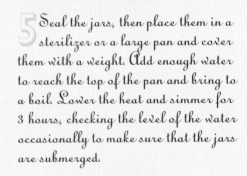

During this time taste last season's pâtés and plan the date for the next production. Careful, as Jacquy is often unavailable!

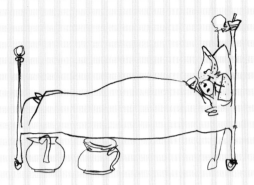

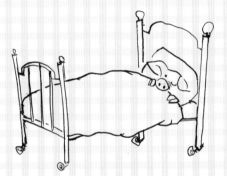

Granny Pig

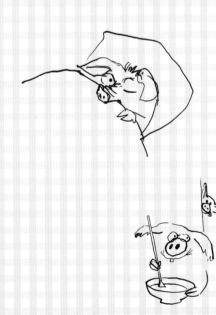

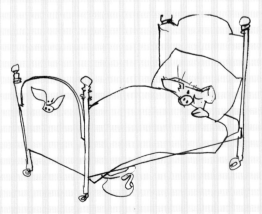

Cabbage Soup

PREPARATION TIME: 20 MINUTES
COOKING TIME: 1¼ HOURS

SERVES 6

scant ½ cup olive oil
1 white cabbage, cored and shredded
¾ cup white wine
3 large potatoes, coarsely chopped
2 onions, coarsely chopped
a pinch of freshly grated nutmeg
6 thick slices of fresh pork belly
3 garlic cloves, thinly sliced
scant 1 cup heavy cream
salt and pepper

Heat 5 tablespoons of the oil in a large pan. Add the cabbage and cook, stirring occasionally, for a few minutes, until softened but not colored. Add the white wine, potatoes, onions, and nutmeg and pour in enough water to cover. Add the pork and bring to a boil, then lower the heat, and simmer gently for about 1 hour, until the meat is tender.

Remove the meat with a slotted spoon. Transfer the soup to a blender or food processor and process until smooth. Season to taste with salt and pepper.

Heat the remaining oil in a small skillet. Add the garlic and cook over low heat, stirring frequently, until it is just beginning to color. If necessary, reheat the soup.

Serve the soup hot in bowls with a swirl of cream and the garlic chips. Serve the belly either in the soup or separately on slices of toasted rustic bread.

Hello to Papily, who adores cabbage soup, especially when there's a lot of bacon and not much cabbage!

Potée

PREPARATION TIME: 30 MINUTES
COOKING TIME: 3 HOURS 10 MINUTES

SERVES 6

1 fresh ham hock or 1 pound bone-in shank portion of a fresh ham
1 onion
1 bouquet garni
1 pound 2 ounces brined spareribs (see below for brining instructions)
1 Morteau sausage (see pages 64 and 65) or other large smoked sausage
6 Toulouse or paysanne sausages (see pages 64 and 65) or other
  country-style sausages or saucissons a'l'ail (see *Sources*)
1 thick slice of smoked slab bacon
1 cabbage, cored and cut into 6 pieces
6 carrots
6 turnip greens
6 small potatoes
1 celery root
3 leeks, halved

Put the ham hock, onion, and bouquet garni in a large flameproof casserole, add water to cover, and bring to a boil. Lower the heat and cook for 2½ hours. Alternatively, cook in a pressure cooker for 45 minutes.

Add the spareribs, both types of sausages, and the bacon and cook for a further 20 minutes. Add all the vegetables and cook for 20 minutes more. Remove and discard the bouquet garni. Remove the Morteau or other large smoked sausage with a slotted spoon, cut it into six pieces, and return to the casserole. Serve hot.

BRINING

The following is a recipe for brining your own meat. You can brine all cuts of pork with this. Pork chops take about 12 hours; an entire loin takes 4 days. Put the cut of meat in a nonreactive container such as a glazed pottery crock, a plastic or stainless steel bowl, or a heavy plastic freezer bag. Fill the container with enough water to cover the meat then pour off the water and measure it. For every three quarts of spring water, add ¾ pound sea salt, ¾ pound brown sugar, 1 tablespoon peppercorns and 2 bay leaves. Stir until the salt and sugar are dissolved. Cover the meat with the solution and refrigerate for at least 12 hours and up to 4 days. Drain and completely dry the meat before using.

pork with lentils

PREPARATION TIME: 20 MINUTES
COOKING TIME: 2 HOURS

SERVES 6

1⅓ cups green lentils, preferably French ones from Puy
2 pounds 11 ounces brined Boston butt (see page 214
  for brining instructions), drained and patted dry
1 Morteau sausage (see pages 64 and 65)
  or other large smoked sausage
½ pound smoked slab bacon
2 carrots
1 onion, studded with 1 clove
1 bouquet garni
2¼ cups dry white wine
scant 1 cup heavy cream
salt and pepper

If you have not brined the Boston Butt yourself, remove the salt from the meat by rinsing it several times. Blanch the meat in a pan of boiling water for a few minutes, then drain.

Put the lentils in a pan, add water to cover, and bring to a boil, then drain, and rinse. Place the lentils, pork, sausage, bacon, carrots, onion, and bouquet garni in a large pan and add enough white wine to cover (if there is insufficient, top up with water). Bring to a boil, then lower the heat, and simmer for 1½ hours.

Transfer two ladlefuls of lentils to a blender or food processor and process to a purée. Stir the purée into the cream. Mix the lentil cream with the rest of the lentils.

Remove the bouquet garni from the pork stew and discard. Remove the pork, sausage, and bacon from the pan and cut each into six portions. Season to taste with salt and pepper and serve, accompanied by the lentils.

Classic pork with lentils

PREPARATION TIME: 30 MINUTES
COOKING TIME: 3 HOURS

SERVES 6

1 brined pork hock (see page 214 for brining instructions),
  drained and patted dry
1 smoked Boston butt
2 bouquets garnis
1 fresh rosemary sprig
6 juniper berries
1 pound 5 ounces brined spareribs (see page 214),
  drained and patted dry
1 Morteau sausage (see pages 64 and 65)
  or other large smoked sausage
1¾ cups green lentils, preferably French ones from Puy
3 carrots, cut into cubes
3 onions, cut into cubes
¾ cup dry white wine

Put the pork hock and Boston butt, one of the bouquets garnis, the rosemary, and juniper berries in a large flameproof casserole. Add water to cover and bring to a boil, then lower the heat, and simmer for 1 hour. Add the spareribs and simmer for a further 30 minutes. Add the sausage and simmer for 30 minutes more. Remove the casserole from the heat and set aside.

Put the lentils in a pan, add water to cover and bring to a boil, then drain, and rinse. Return the lentils to the pan, add the remaining bouquet garni, the carrots, onions, and white wine, and pour in sufficient water to cover. Bring to a boil, then lower the heat, and simmer for 30 minutes.

Remove the meat from the casserole and slice. Drain the lentil mixture and discard the bouquet garni. Put the meat and lentil mixture in a pan, add two ladlefuls of the meat cooking liquid, and simmer gently for 15 minutes. Serve hot.

Grandma Barbe's Roast pork

PREPARATION TIME: 15 MINUTES
COOKING TIME: 2 HOURS

SERVES 6

6 tablespoons olive oil
2½-pound boneless pork loin cut from the tip (not center cut)
12 pearl onions
1 pound 2 ounces carrots
2¼ cups dry white wine
2¼ pounds waxy potatoes, halved
¼ cup sweet butter
1 bouquet garni
3 garlic cloves
1 bunch of fresh parsley
sea salt

Heat the olive oil a flameproof casserole. Add the pork and cook over medium heat, turning occasionally, for 8–10 minutes, until golden brown all over. Lower the heat, cover, and cook, turning occasionally, for 1½ hours.

Peel the onions and cut off the tops. Peel the carrots and cut the ends at an angle.

Pour the white wine into the casserole and add the onions, carrots, potatoes, butter, and bouquet garni. Replace the lid and simmer for about 30 minutes, until the potatoes are tender.

Meanwhile, coarsely chop the garlic and parsley together.

Remove the bouquet garni from the casserole and discard. Season the roast with sea salt and sprinkle the garlic and parsley mixture on the potatoes before serving.

Larded and studded roast

PREPARATION TIME: 15 MINUTES
COOKING TIME: 1¾ HOURS

SERVES 6

6 garlic cloves
2½-pound boneless center-cut pork loin
¼ cup sweet butter, chilled and cut into thin sticks
3 fresh rosemary sprigs, cut into small pieces
10 thin slices of fresh pork belly
kitchen twine

Preheat the oven to 250°F. Peel the garlic and cut each clove into four. Make small incisions in the pork loin with a small sharp knife. Insert the sticks of butter, garlic slices, and pieces of rosemary in the cuts. Wrap up the loin in the slices of fresh pork belly, tying them in place with kitchen twine.

Place the rolled pork in a roasting pan and cook over medium heat, turning occasionally, for about 10 minutes, until evenly browned. Sprinkle any remaining rosemary on top, then transfer to the oven, and roast, basting frequently, for 1½ hours.

Granny Pig

Pork chops with shallots

PREPARATION TIME: 5 MINUTES
COOKING TIME: 20 MINUTES

SERVES 6

¼ cup sweet butter
8 shallots, chopped
6 bone-in, center-cut pork chops
10 fresh thyme sprigs, preferably in flower
sea salt
coarsely ground black pepper

Melt 1½ tablespoons of the butter in a pan. Add the shallots and cook, stirring frequently, over high heat for 8–10 minutes, until golden brown.

Melt the remaining butter in a skillet. Add the chops and cook over high heat for 5 minutes on each side, or until cooked through and the juices have caramelized.

Season with sea salt and coarsely ground black pepper. Mix the thyme with the shallots. Serve the chops with the shallots immediately.

Pork Boston butt with milk

PREPARATION TIME: 5 MINUTES
COOKING TIME: 2 HOURS

SERVES 6

1 Boston butt, weighing about 3¼ lb
8¾ cups fresh whole milk
3 garlic cloves
1 fresh thyme sprig
1 fresh rosemary sprig
2 bay leaves

Preheat the oven to 350°F. Put the pork in a large casserole, pour in the milk. and add the garlic, thyme, rosemary, and bay leaves.

Cover the casserole and bake, for about 2 hours, until the milk has almost completely evaporated. Discard the herbs. The pork may be eaten cold or hot, served with the milk 'jam' taken from the base of the casserole.

Roast rack of piglet with polenta fries

PREPARATION TIME: 1 HOUR
COOKING TIME: 1 HOUR 25 MINUTES

SERVES 6

4 cups fresh whole milk
scant 1½ cups polenta or corn meal
4 eggs, lightly beaten
6 tablespoons olive oil
1 rack of 6 chops from a piglet
2 lemon grass stalks, coarsely chopped
6 garlic cloves, coarsely chopped
3 shallots, coarsely chopped
2-inch piece of fresh ginger root, coarsely chopped
1 fresh thyme sprig
¾ cup white wine
¼ cup sweet butter

Pour the milk into a pan and bring to a boil. Add the polenta in a steady stream and cook over low heat, stirring constantly, until the polenta comes away from the sides of the pan. This will take 20–30 minutes for ordinary polenta and about 5 minutes for quick-cook polenta. Stir in the eggs and cook for a further 10 minutes. Spread out the polenta in a layer about ½ inch thick on a sheet of waxed paper and chill in the refrigerator until set.

Preheat the oven to 325°F.

Heat the olive oil in a roasting pan, add the rack of chops, and cook over medium heat, turning occasionally, for about 10 minutes, until golden brown all over. Add the lemon grass, garlic, shallots, ginger, and thyme and pour in the wine. Transfer to the oven and roast, basting frequently, for 1¼ hours.

Cut thick fries from the polenta. Melt the butter in a skillet, add the polenta fries, and cook over low heat, turning occasionally, until golden brown.

Transfer the rack to a serving dish, surround with the polenta fries, and serve immediately.

Rack of pork with hard cider and apple butter

PREPARATION TIME: 15 MINUTES
COOKING TIME: 1½ HOURS

SERVES 6

1 rack of pork with 6 chops
2¼ cups hard cider
6 Granny Smith or other tart eating apples
3 onions, sliced
a pinch of ground cinnamon
a pinch of ground ginger
7 tablespoons sweet butter, chilled

Cook the rack in a flameproof casserole over medium heat, turning occasionally, until golden brown all over. Baste with a little of the hard cider, lower the heat, cover, and cook for 1 hour, basting frequently with more hard cider.

Peel and core the apples, then cut into fourths. Add them to the casserole with the onions, the remaining hard cider, and the spices and cook over low heat for a further 5–10 minutes, until the apples and onions have softened.

Remove the rack from the casserole, tent with foil, and let stand for 10 minutes. Add the butter to the casserole and beat it into the apple mixture. Cut the rack into separate chops and serve with the hard cider and apple butter.

Whole ham with honey and cloves

SOAKING AND MARINATING TIME: 24 HOURS
PREPARATION TIME: 30 MINUTES
COOKING TIME: 1 HOUR PER 1 KG HAM, PLUS 1 HOUR

SERVES MANY HUNGRY PEOPLE

1 brined whole ham (see page 214 for
  brining instructions)
4 carrots
1 leek, green part only
3 onions
2 fresh thyme sprigs
2 bay leaves
20 cloves
¼ cup sweet butter

FOR THE MARINADE

2 tablespoons Quatre-épices (see page 154)
2 tablespoons curry powder
4 tablespoons sugar
2 tablespoons honey
2 tablespoons olive oil
½ bottle (1⅔ cups) Côtes du Rhône
  or Shiraz wine
scant ½ cup cognac or brandy
scant 1 cup port

If you have not brined the ham yourself, place it in a large bowl, add water to cover, and let soak during the day before you intend to cook it.

Drain the ham, pat dry with paper towels and make a note of the weight of the ham. Combine all the ingredients for the marinade in a nonmetallic dish. Add the ham, turning to coat. Cover and let marinate overnight.

Next day, put the carrots, leek, onions, thyme, and bay leaves in a large pan. Drain the ham, reserving the marinade. Add the ham to the pan, pour in water to cover, and bring to a boil, then lower the heat, and simmer gently, allowing 30 minutes per pound.

Preheat the oven to 350°F. Drain the ham, cut a crisscross pattern in the skin, and stud it with the cloves. Place the ham in a roasting pan, pour the reserved marinade over it, and roast, basting frequently, for 1 hour, until golden.

Remove the ham from the roasting pan. Place the pan over low heat and beat in the butter. Pour the sauce into a sauceboat and serve with the ham.

Slow-cooked ham hock with red cabbage

PREPARATION TIME: 20 MINUTES
COOKING TIME: 3 HOURS

SERVES 6

4 tablespoons olive oil
2 onions, sliced
1 lemon grass stalk, sliced
2 garlic cloves, chopped
generous ½ cup chopped smoked bacon
3½ ounces spicy Spanish chorizo (see pages 68 and 69),
  cut into thin batons, or Mexican chorizo (see *Sources*)
  cooked, drained, and cut up
1 red cabbage, about 2¼ pounds, cored and sliced
4 cups white wine
2 fresh ham hocks or 1 small shank end of a fresh ham
1 tablespoon brown sugar
1 teaspoon ground cumin

Heat the oil in a large pan. Add the onions, lemon grass, garlic, bacon, and chorizo and cook over low heat, stirring occasionally, for about 10 minutes, until golden brown. Stir in the red cabbage and white wine. Place the ham hocks in the pan, pour in sufficient water to cover, and add the sugar and cumin. Cover and cook over low heat for about 3 hours, checking frequently that the cabbage hasn't stuck to the base of the pan and adding more water, if necessary.

When the meat is cooked – when the flesh comes away from the bone – bring the remaining cooking liquid to a boil and cook until it has evaporated. Serve the ham hocks whole, covered with the red cabbage.

Glazed pork hocks with warm potato salad and Sarrassou cheese

PREPARATION TIME: 3 HOURS 20 MINUTES
MARINATING TIME: 12 HOURS
COOKING TIME: 20 MINUTES

SERVES 6

2 fresh pork hocks or 1 small shank end of a fresh ham
1 tablespoon soy sauce
1 tablespoon brown sugar
1 tablespoon tomato ketchup
3 tablespoons vegetable oil
10 potatoes
1 bunch of fresh chives, chopped
2 shallots, chopped
9 ounces Sarrassou cheese, fromage blanc (see *Sources*),
  or ricotta
1 teaspoon chestnut or other honey
2 tablespoons canola oil
salt

The day before you intend to serve, put the pork hocks in a large pan, add water to cover, and bring to a boil. Lower the heat and simmer for 3 hours, until very tender. Drain well.

Combine the soy sauce, sugar, ketchup, and vegetable oil in a bowl. Brush the pork hocks all over with this marinade and let stand in a cool place for 12 hours.

The next day preheat the oven to 350°F. Cook the potatoes in a pan of salted boiling water for about 20 minutes, until tender but still firm. Meanwhile, combine the chives, shallots, cheese, honey, and canola oil; set aside.

Place the pork hocks in a roasting pan and spoon the marinade over them. Roast, basting frequently with the marinade, for 20 minutes, until heated through and golden brown.

Place the glazed pork hocks on a serving plate. Drain the potatoes, cut into rounds, and spoon the cheese mixture over them. Serve immediately.

Stuffed cabbage

PREPARATION TIME: 20 MINUTES
COOKING TIME: 2¼ HOURS

SERVES 6

1 white cabbage
6 tablespoons olive oil
2 shallots, chopped
2 garlic cloves, chopped
1½ cups chopped cremini mushrooms
scant 1 cup chopped preserved chestnuts
generous 1 cup chopped cooked pork
9 ounces bulk (breakfast) sausage, skins removed
1½ tablespoons sweet butter
¾ cup white wine
salt and pepper

Core the cabbage and separate the leaves. Select 12 large leaves, blanch them in salted boiling water for 1 minute, then drain, and refresh in cold water.

Chop the remaining cabbage leaves. Heat the oil in a large pan. Add the shallots, garlic, mushrooms, chestnuts, and chopped cabbage and cook over low heat, stirring occasionally, for 5–10 minutes, until softened. Combine the pork and sausagemeat in a bowl and stir in the cabbage mixture. Season with salt and pepper.

Reassemble the cabbage, alternating the stuffing and leaves, and place it in a large lidded flameproof casserole or earthenware pot. Add water to the pot to come to a depth of 2 inches, and cover with the lid. Cook the cabbage in the oven for 1½ hours, adding water as necessary during cooking. Drain the cooking water, then add the butter and pour the white wine over. Bring to the boil on the stovetop, then lower the heat, cover and simmer, basting frequently, for 30 minutes.

Alsace pork stew

PREPARATION TIME: 20 MINUTES
MARINATING TIME: 12 HOURS
COOKING TIME: 3 HOURS

SERVES 6

2 cooked pig's feet
1 pound 5 ounces boneless brined Boston butt (see page 214 for
 brining instructions), drained, patted dry and cut into cubes
1 pound 5 ounces brined pork spareribs (see page 214), drained,
 separated, and patted dry
11 ounces smoked slab bacon, cut into cubes
2 carrots, thinly sliced
2 garlic cloves, chopped
2 shallots, chopped
2 celery stalks, thinly sliced
2¼ cups Riesling wine
⅓ cup lard
2¼ pounds potatoes, thickly sliced
1 pound 2 ounces onions, thickly sliced
1¼ cup all-purpose flour

Remove the meat from the bones of the pig's feet and cut into cubes. Put all the meat, the carrots, garlic, shallots, celery, and wine in a large dish and mix well. Let marinate in a cool place for 12 hours.

Preheat the oven to 400°F. Grease a lidded earthenware casserole with the lard. Put half the potatoes in the base and cover with half the onions. Drain the meat and vegetables from the marinade and place them on top of the onions, then add the remaining onions and potatoes. Pour in the marinade.

Cover the dish or casserole with the lid. Mix the flour with water to a paste and spread it around the lid to seal. Bake for 1 hour, then lower the oven temperature to 325°F and cook for a further 2 hours. Serve straight from the dish, breaking the seal at the table.

Super Maxi Royale Choucroute

PREPARATION TIME: 30 MINUTES
COOKING TIME: 40 MINUTES

SERVES 6

3¼ pounds cooked sauerkraut
2¼ cups Riesling wine
12 small potatoes
Frankfurter sausage
Montbéliard sausage (see pages 64 and 65) or
  smoked Mexican-American style chorizo (see *Sources*)
cumin-flavored sausage
Strasbourg sausage (see pages 64 and 65) or hotdog
Morteau sausage (see pages 64 and 65) or other
  large smoked sausage
sausage confit
garlic-flavored sausage
cinnamon-flavored blood sausage
smoked bacon
fresh pork belly
pork hock
pork ribs
brined Boston butt (see page 214 for brining instructions)

To make a good choucroute, take one good charcutier!

Boil the potatoes in water for 20–25 minutes.

Meanwhile, preheat the sauerkraut in a sturdy flameproof casserole with the Riesling. Reheat the meat in hot water, then arrange on the sauerkraut in the casserole.

Cover and cook for a further 15 minutes. Add the cooked potatoes and serve.

CHOUCROUTE

There is no fixed recipe for Choucroute but the basic ingredients are sauerkraut (sour cabbage), potatoes, white wine and different types of meat, including all or some of the following: sausages, salted meats, fresh meat on the bone and bacon. It can be served as a side or main dish.

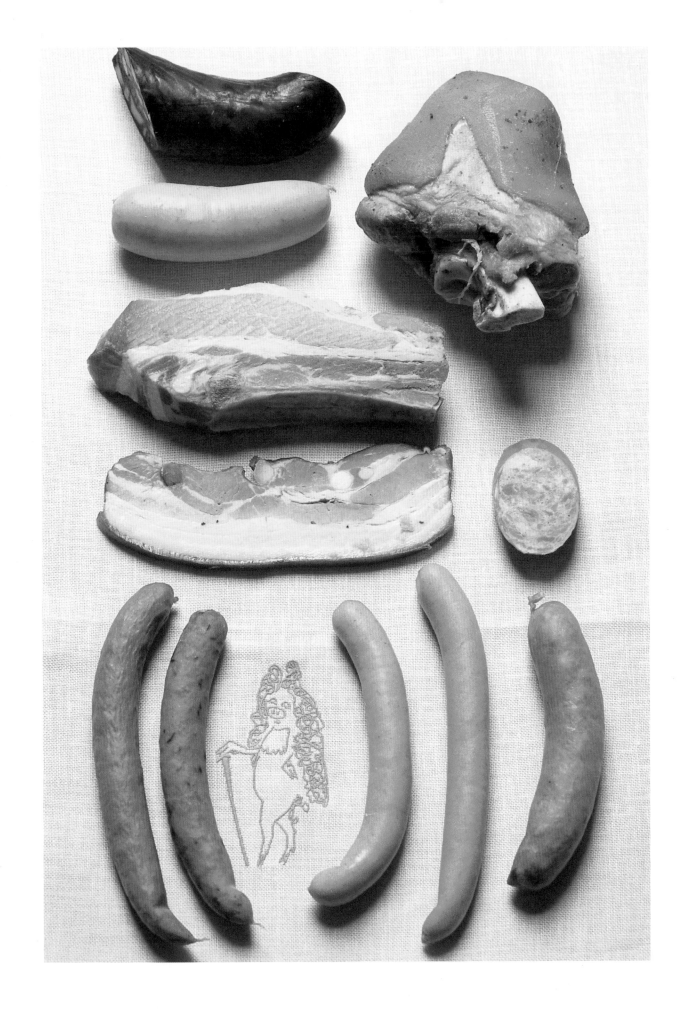

Pork ragoût with sage and brown beans

SOAKING TIME: 24 HOURS
PREPARATION TIME: 20 MINUTES
COOKING TIME: 2 HOURS

SERVES 6

2¾ cups dried brown beans, cranberry beans, or pintos,
  soaked in cold water for 24 hours
1 bouquet garni
2½ tablespoons fresh lard
2¼ pounds boneless pork loin, cut into large cubes
2 onions, sliced
3 garlic cloves, crushed
1 tablespoon all-purpose flour
2¼ cups white wine
20 fresh sage leaves
6 tomatoes, peeled
1 tablespoon tomato paste
salt and pepper

Drain the beans and place them in a pan. Add water to cover and bring to a boil, then drain, and rinse. Return the beans to the pan, add the bouquet garni and water to cover, and bring to a boil. Lower the heat and simmer for 1½ hours.

Melt the lard in a pan. Add the pork, onions, and garlic and cook over medium heat, stirring frequently, for about 10 minutes, until the pork is evenly browned. Stir in the flour and cook, stirring constantly, for 2 minutes, then gradually stir in the wine. Add the sage leaves, tomatoes, and tomato paste and simmer for 30 minutes.

Drain the beans, reserving a little of the cooking liquid. Stir them into the meat mixture, adding the reserved cooking liquid, if necessary. Simmer for a further 30 minutes, then season to taste with salt and pepper, and serve.

Spiced pork belly confit

PREPARATION TIME: 20 MINUTES
COOKING TIME: 2¼ HOURS

SERVES 6

6 pieces of fresh pork belly, each weighing about ½ pound
4 cups white wine
1 tablespoon glace de veau
1 teaspoon paprika
1 teaspoon curry powder
1 teaspoon saffron threads
1 teaspoon ground ginger
1 teaspoon ground cumin
2 tablespoons brown sugar
3 garlic cloves, chopped
½ cup sweet butter
6 large potatoes, cut into thin rounds

Preheat the oven to 350°F. Heat a griddle pan, add the pieces of pork, and cook over medium heat, turning occasionally, until golden brown all over. Add the white wine and stir, scraping up any sediment from the base of the pan, then transfer the mixture to an ovenproof dish.

Bring 4 cups water to a boil in a pan. Stir in the glace de veau, paprika, curry powder, saffron, ginger, cumin, sugar, and garlic and pour into the dish. Place in the oven and cook, basting and turning the meat frequently, for about 2 hours, until almost all the liquid has evaporated and the pork is very tender. If necessary, add more water during cooking.

Melt the butter in a nonstick pan and add the potato rounds arranged in the form of rosettes. Cook over high heat, turning once, until the rosettes are golden brown.

Place a slice of pork and a potato rosette on each of six plates and serve immediately.

Pork pot-au-feu with vegetables

PREPARATION TIME: 45 MINUTES
COOKING TIME: 1 HOUR

SERVES 6

6 slices of brined Boston butt (see page 214 for
  brining instructions), drained and patted dry
6 pieces of fresh pork belly
3 onions
6 small leeks
6 Jerusalem artichokes
3 parsnips, halved
3 turnips or rutabagas, halved
6 carrot tops
6 turnip tops
1 bouquet garni
1 tablespoon vegetable oil
2-inch piece of fresh ginger root, cut into thin batons
1½ teaspoons grated or finely chopped horseradish
scant ½ cup heavy cream
1 jar of cornichons (miniature French cucumber pickles)
coarse salt

Put the meat, onions, and leeks in a flameproof casserole and add enough water to cover. Bring
to a boil, then lower the heat, and simmer for 30 minutes.

Add the Jerusalem artichokes, parsnips, turnips, carrot tops, turnip tops, and bouquet garni and
cook for a further 30 minutes.

Heat the oil in a small skillet, add the ginger and cook over high heat, stirring constantly, for
a few minutes, until golden brown. Combine the horseradish and cream in a bowl. Place the
cornichons in a serving bowl.

Place a slice of pork and a piece of belly side in each of six soup plates. Divide the vegetables
among them and sprinkle with the fried ginger. Serve the coarse salt, cornichons, and
horseradish cream separately.

Grandmother's pig's cheek bourguignon

PREPARATION TIME: 15 MINUTES
COOKING TIME: 1½ HOURS

SERVES 6

2½ pounds pig's cheeks (meat only), halved
2 onions, sliced
2 garlic cloves, crushed
generous ½ cup chopped smoked bacon
2 tablespoons all-purpose flour
4 cups Côtes du Rhône or Shiraz wine
1 bouquet garni
2¼ cups water
1¾ pounds carrots
¼ cup sweet butter, chilled
salt and pepper

Heat a heavy flameproof casserole. Add the cheeks and cook over medium heat, turning occasionally, until golden brown all over. Lower the heat, add the onions, garlic, and bacon, and cook, stirring frequently, for 5 minutes, until the onions are softened and the bacon is beginning to color. Stir in the flour and cook, stirring constantly, for 2 minutes, then gradually stir in the red wine. Add the bouquet garni, pour in the water, and bring to a boil, then simmer for 1 hour.

Peel the carrots, slice thickly at an angle, then add them to the casserole. Simmer for a further 30 minutes, until the meat is tender and the sauce is thick enough to coat the back of a spoon. Season with salt and pepper.

Remove and discard the bouquet garni. Remove the meat and carrots with a slotted spoon and keep warm. If necessary, bring the sauce to a boil and reduce slightly. Beat in the chilled butter and bring to a boil, whisking constantly. Return the meat and carrots to the casserole and heat through. Serve immediately.

BOURGUIGNON

Beef bourguignon is a very well known French dish consisting of beef stewed with red wine, garlic, vegetables and a bouquet garni. The recipe above is a delicious variation.

Smoked Boston butt with cabbage salad

PREPARATION TIME: 20 MINUTES
COOKING TIME: 1½ HOURS

SERVES 6

1 smoked Boston butt
1 carrot
1 leek
1 onion
1 bouquet garni
scant ½ cup olive oil
scant ½ cup sunflower oil
1 egg
1 tablespoon red wine vinegar
1 tablespoon Dijon mustard
10 cornichons (miniature French cucumber pickles), diced
1 shallot, diced
1 bunch of fresh chives, thinly sliced
1 tablespoon capers
1 white cabbage, cored and shredded
salt and pepper

Put the pork, carrot, leek, onion, and bouquet garni in a flameproof casserole, add water to cover, and bring to a boil. Lower the heat and simmer for 1½ hours.

Meanwhile, combine the olive and sunflower oils in a pitcher. Beat the egg in a bowl, then gradually whisk in the oil, 1–2 teaspoons at a time, until about one-fourth has been incorporated. Whisk in the vinegar, then whisk in the remaining oil, adding it in a thin steady stream. Stir in the mustard.

Stir the cornichons, shallot, chives, and capers into the mayonnaise and season with salt and pepper. Toss the cabbage in the mayonnaise.

Remove the meat from the casserole and carve into slices. Serve warm with the cabbage salad handed separately.

Granny Pig

Roast pork with herbs and baby peas

PREPARATION TIME: 15 MINUTES
COOKING TIME: 1¾ HOURS

SERVES 6

4 tablespoons olive oil
2½ pounds center-cut pork loin
generous 1 cup chopped smoked bacon
3 shallots, halved
4 garlic cloves, crushed
¾ cup white wine
8 fresh sage leaves
2 fresh thyme sprigs
1 fresh rosemary sprig
2 bay leaves
6 pearl onions
9 cups frozen baby peas
2 tablespoons sweet butter
3 fresh tarragon sprigs, chopped
6 fresh basil leaves
sea salt

Heat the olive oil in a flameproof casserole. Add the pork and cook over medium heat, turning occasionally, for 8–10 minutes, until golden brown all over.

Lower the heat, add the bacon, shallots, and garlic, and cook, stirring frequently, for about 10 minutes, until the shallots are softened and lightly colored. Pour in the white wine and add the sage leaves, thyme, rosemary, bay leaves, and onions. Cover and simmer, basting frequently, for 1½ hours. If the casserole seems to be drying out, add a little water.

Toward the end of the cooking time, cook the peas in salted boiling water for 5 minutes, then drain. Add the butter, tarragon, and basil to the casserole and stir in the peas. Season to taste with sea salt and serve.

Roast pork with sage

PREPARATION TIME: 20 MINUTES
COOKING TIME: 2 HOURS

SERVES 6

6 tablespoons olive oil, plus extra for drizzling
1 pork loin, about 2½ pounds
2¼ pounds large potatoes, sliced
1 pound 2 ounces onions, sliced
generous ½ cup chopped fresh pork belly
1 fresh sage sprig
2¼ cups dry white wine
3 bay leaves
salt and pepper

Preheat the oven to 350°F. Heat the olive oil in a flameproof casserole, add the pork, and cook over medium heat, turning occasionally, for 8–10 minutes, until golden brown all over. Cover and roast in the oven, basting frequently, for 1 hour.

Combine the potatoes, onions, belly, and sage leaves and season with salt and pepper. Add this mixture to the casserole and pour in the white wine. Add the bay leaves.

Re-cover the casserole and cook in the oven for a further 45 minutes, until the vegetables are tender. Drizzle with olive oil and serve.

Granny Pig

Andouillettes with morels and vin jaune

PREPARATION TIME: 10 MINUTES
COOKING TIME: 30 MINUTES

SERVES 6

2 ounces morels or other dried mushrooms
2 tablespoons vegetable oil
1 garlic clove, chopped
3 shallots, chopped
scant 1 cup vin jaune (a unique wine made from savagnin grapes)
  or sherry-like wine
1¾ cups heavy cream
6 Troyes andouillettes (see page 66) or other tripe sausages
  (see *Sources*)

Put the mushrooms in a bowl, add lukewarm water to cover, and let soak for 30 minutes, then drain. Preheat the oven to 250°F.

Heat the oil in a skillet. Add the garlic and shallots and cook over low heat, stirring occasionally, for 5 minutes, until softened. Add the mushrooms and cook for a further 5 minutes. Stir in the vin jaune, scraping up any sediment from the base of the pan with a wooden spoon. Bring to a boil and reduce slightly, then stir in the cream, and heat through but do not let boil.

Place an andouillette in each of six individual porcelain gratin dishes, divide the mushroom cream among them, and bake in the oven for 15 minutes, until the sausages are heated through. Serve immediately.

CLASS AAAAA

The quality of this dish depends above all on the quality of the ingredients. Ideally, use an AAAAA – Association Amicale des Amateurs d'Authentiques Andouillettes (Association of Friends for the Appreciation of Genuine Andouillettes) – Troyes andouillette, made exclusively from seasoned pork.

l'ivrogne Andouillettes

PREPARATION TIME: 10 MINUTES
COOKING TIME: 1 HOUR

SERVES 6

generous ½ cup chopped fresh pork belly
4 onions, sliced
4 teaspoons brandy
2¼ cups Côtes du Rhône or Shiraz wine
1 beef bouillon cube
1½ tablespoons sweet butter
1 teaspoon all-purpose flour
6 Troyes andouillettes (see page 66 and 258) or
  other tripe sausages (see *Sources*)

Preheat the oven to 250°F. Heat a heavy pan, add the belly and onions, and cook over medium heat, stirring occasionally, for about 10 minutes, until they are well browned. Add the brandy and heat for a few seconds, then ignite. When the flames have died down, stir in the wine, scraping up any sediment from the base of the pan with a wooden spoon. Bring to a boil and reduce by half.

Mix the bouillon cube with 2¼ cups hot water and add to the pan. Bring back to a boil and reduce by half. Blend the butter and flour to a paste with a fork, then beat the paste into the sauce in small pieces, one at a time. Simmer for 5 minutes.

Place a sausage in each of six individual porcelain gratin dishes and divide the sauce among them.

Bake in the oven for 15 minutes, until the sausages are heated through. Serve immediately, with your favorite roasted vegetables alongside.

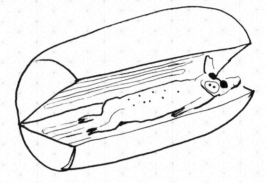

Barbecued pork

fumé

zippo

Tatoo

Marinades for 6 slices of boneless pork

SPICED TOMATO

2 tablespoons tomato ketchup
2 tablespoons soy sauce
2 tablespoons lemon juice
2 tablespoons sugar
2 tablespoons vegetable oil
2 garlic cloves, crushed

LEMON GRASS AND COCONUT MILK

1 lemon grass stalk, chopped
2 garlic cloves, crushed
1 shallot, chopped
4 tablespoons coconut milk
2 tablespoons vegetable oil
1 tablespoon dry unsweetened shredded coconut
1 teaspoon curry powder

MUSTARD, OLIVE OIL, AND OREGANO

3 tablespoons Meaux or other grain mustard
4 tablespoons olive oil
1 teaspoon dried oregano
1 teaspoon ground cumin

MAPLE SYRUP

3 tablespoons maple syrup
3 tablespoons vegetable oil
1 tablespoon white port
2 tablespoons ground hazelnuts

GINGER AND GARLIC

1 tablespoon chopped fresh ginger root
2 garlic cloves, chopped
3 fresh cilantro sprigs, chopped
3 tablespoons olive oil
1 tablespoon brown sugar
2 tablespoons white wine

Barbecued pork

Crispy pork

PREPARATION TIME: 5 MINUTES
COOKING TIME: 5 MINUTES

SERVES 6

6 thick slices of fresh pork belly, each at least ¼ inch thick
6 thick slices of smoked slab bacon, each at least ¼ inch thick
spices, to taste

Roll the pork belly in a mixture of spices to coat (feel free to use your imagination when choosing which spices to use).

Cook on a barbecue grill as high as possible above the embers, as the melting fat causes flames which could burn your meat.

Barbecued pork

Breaded feet, ears, and tails with herbs

PREPARATION TIME: 5 MINUTES
COOKING TIME: 10 MINUTES

SERVES 6

6 cooked pig's tails
dried herbes de Provence, for coating
3 cooked and breaded pig's feet, halved
3 cooked pig's ears

The feet, ears, and tails have to be cooked before grilling on the barbecue. A number of butchers sell them precooked. Packets of dried herbes de Provence, consisting of thyme, rosemary, bay leaves, basil, and savory, are widely available from supermarkets, or you can make your own combination.

Roll the tails in the herbes de Provence and cook all the meat slowly on the barbecue until it is just browned.

Barbecued pork

Spareribs with barbecue sauce

PREPARATION TIME: 20 MINUTES
MARINATING TIME: 12 HOURS
COOKING TIME: 20 MINUTES PLUS 55 MINUTES THE DAY BEFORE

SERVES 6

4½ pounds pork spareribs
7 ounces tomato ketchup
2 tablespoons dark soy sauce
2 tablespoons Maggi or other similar seasoning
  (or another 2 tablespoons soy sauce)
1 teaspoon cognac or brandy
2 tablespoons sugar
4 garlic cloves, chopped
2 tablespoons vegetable oil
1 teaspoon coarsely ground black pepper

Separate the ribs by cutting between them with a sharp knife. Place in a large pan, add water to cover, and bring to a boil. Lower the heat and simmer for 45 minutes.

Meanwhile, combine the ketchup, soy sauce, Maggi, brandy or cognac, sugar, garlic, oil, and pepper in a large bowl. Drain the ribs, refresh in cold water, pat dry, and add them to bowl, turning to coat. Cover and set aside in a cool place for 12 hours.

Cook the ribs on the barbecue for 20 minutes, turning frequently and brushing with any remaining sauce, until caramelized.

Pork loin and bell pepper kabobs

PREPARATION TIME: 20 MINUTES
COOKING TIME: 15 MINUTES

SERVES 6

2¼ pounds pork loin, taken from the tip (not center-cut)
1 red bell pepper, halved and seeded
1 green bell pepper, halved and seeded
1 yellow bell pepper, halved and seeded
2 onions
1 tablespoon sugar
1 tablespoon balsamic vinegar
2 tablespoons olive oil
1 tablespoon ras el hanout (see below)
mixed salad greens, to serve

Cut the pork into 36 large cubes and cut each bell pepper into 12 squares. Cut the onions into 36 small wedges.

Put the sugar and vinegar in a small pan and cook over low heat, stirring until the sugar has dissolved. Pour into a bowl and stir in the olive oil and ras el hanout. Add the pork cubes, turning to coat.

Thread the pork, onions, and bell peppers alternately on to 12 kabob skewers. (If using wooden or bamboo skewers, soak them in cold water for 30 minutes first to prevent charring.) Cook on the barbecue, frequently turning and brushing the meat with the marinade, for 12–15 minutes, until cooked through and tender. Serve with mixed salad greens.

RAS EL HANOUT

Ras el hanout is a North African spice mix that includes cardamom, cumin, ginger, cinnamon, cloves, turmeric, coriander, nutmeg, and chili—among other spices. It is available from gourmet grocers and Middle Eastern stores.

tenderloin Kabobs

PREPARATION TIME: 20 MINUTES
COOKING TIME: 30 MINUTES

SERVES 6

6 large potatoes
3 small pork tenderloins, total weight about 2½ pounds
18 thin slices of smoked bacon
18 fresh rosemary sprigs
2 shallots, chopped
10 fresh chives, chopped
⅔ cup slightly salted butter, at room temperature

Prick the potatoes, wrap them individually in foil, and place in the embers of the barbecue for 30 minutes.

Meanwhile, cut each tenderloin into six pieces the same size. Wrap a slice of bacon around the side of each piece and secure with a rosemary sprig. Thread three pieces of pork on each of six skewers passing the skewers through the bacon. Grill the kabobs on the barbecue, turning once or twice, for 8 minutes.

Beat the shallots and chives into the butter with a fork.

Unwrap the potatoes, cut them open, and place one on each of six plates with a pork skewer. Spread plenty of shallot butter over the kabobs and the potatoes and serve.

Ash-cooked sausage with Saint Joseph wine

PREPARATION TIME: 10 MINUTES
COOKING TIME: 45 MINUTES

SERVES 6

2 large fresh sausages, such as sweet Italian link sausages
 (see *Sources*)
1²/₃ cups Saint Joseph or Shiraz wine
2 fresh thyme sprigs
2 shallots, chopped

Make two foil packets, each with three layers of foil, large enough to hold the sausages.
Prick the sausages with a fork, place each in a packet, and add the wine, shallots, and thyme.

Seal the packets securely and cook under the ashes of the barbecue for 45 minutes.

Cut the sausages into rounds and pour over the Saint Joseph sauce from the packets.

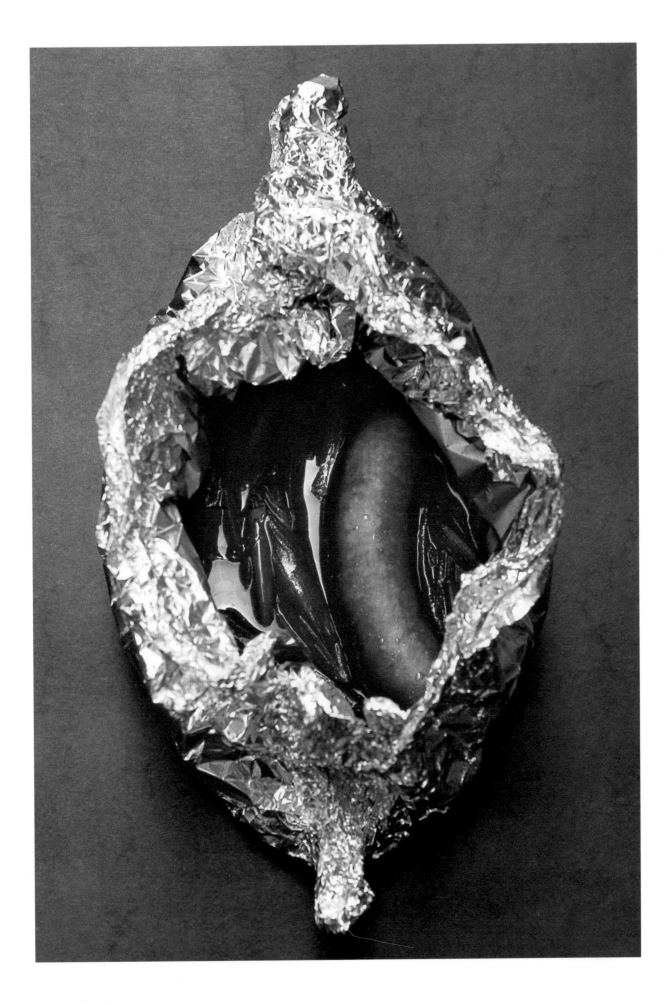

Barbecued suckling pig

PREPARATION TIME: 45 MINUTES
COOKING TIME: 3 HOURS

SERVES 12

1 suckling pig, 5 to 6 weeks old
10 shallots, chopped
10 garlic cloves, chopped
2⅓ cups chopped smoked bacon
7 ounces country-style white bread, soaked in heavy cream
generous ⅓ cup Dijon mustard
3 eggs
1 bunch of fresh parsley, chopped
20 fresh sage leaves, chopped
scant 1 cup olive oil

FOR THE BASTING LIQUID

4 cups white wine
2¼ cups olive oil
scant ¼ cup Dijon mustard

Ask your butcher to prepare the pig and save the liver and heart for you.

Place all the remaining ingredients with the liver and heart in a bowl, and mix together well. Spoon this stuffing into the pig and sew up the cavity with trussing thread. Tie the feet underneath the pig with wire and cover the ears with foil to prevent them from burning.

Whisk together all the ingredients for the basting liquid in a bowl. Place the pig on a spit over the barbecue and cook, basting frequently, for 3 hours.

Barbecued pork

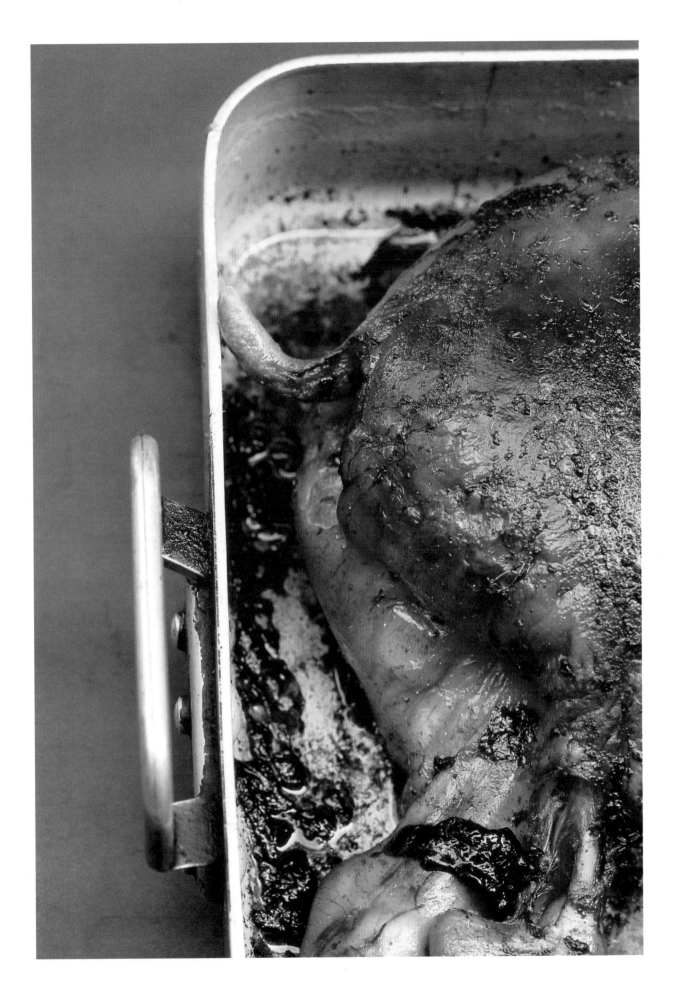

A piggy party

Celery root cream with bacon

PREPARATION TIME: 45 MINUTES
COOKING TIME: 45 MINUTES

SERVES 6

1 slice of dry-cured ham, such as prosciutto
2 tablespoons olive oil
1 onion, chopped
1 celery root, cut into cubes
2 large potatoes, cut into cubes
1 leek, white part only, chopped
a pinch of freshly grated nutmeg
scant ½ cup heavy cream
scant 1 cup fresh whole milk
6 thin slices of smoked bacon

Preheat the oven to 250°F. Place the prosciutto in an ovenproof dish and dry out in the oven for 30 minutes, until crisp, then crumble, and set aside.

Heat the olive oil in a large pan. Add the onion and cook over low heat, stirring occasionally, for about 10 minutes, until light golden brown. Increase the heat to medium, add the celery root, potatoes, leek, and nutmeg, pour in water to cover, and bring to a boil. Lower the heat and simmer for 30 minutes.

Transfer the vegetables and cooking liquid to a blender and process to a purée. Return to the pan, stir in the cream, and season lightly with salt and pepper. Preheat the broiler.

Transfer scant 1 cup of the soup to another pan, add the milk, and heat to just below boiling point, whisking with a hand-held blender until frothy.

Broil the bacon for 2–4 minutes on each side and reheat the soup, but do not let it boil. Ladle the soup into serving bowls, top with the frothy mousse, sprinkle with the crumbled ham, and add a slice of bacon to each.

A piggy party

Pork broth with sesame seeds

PREPARATION TIME: 45 MINUTES
COOKING TIME: 2¼ HOURS

SERVES 6

6 tablespoons olive oil
4 onions, thinly sliced
2 leeks, thinly sliced
6 carrots, thinly sliced
2 celery stalks, thinly sliced
1 bouquet garni
1 bunch of fresh parsley, finely chopped
2 lemon grass stalks
2 small pork tenderloins, total weight about 1¾ pounds
4 tablespoons sesame seeds
a dash of sesame oil
1 bunch of fresh cilantro

Heat 4 tablespoons of the olive oil in a large pan. Add the onions, leeks, carrots, and celery and cook over low heat, stirring occasionally, for 5–8 minutes, until softened. Increase the heat to medium, pour in 8¾ cups water, add the bouquet garni, parsley, and lemon grass, and bring to a boil. Lower the heat and cook for about 2 hours, until the liquid has reduced by half.

Meanwhile, cut the pork into strips. Heat the remaining olive oil in a wok or skillet, add the pork, and stir-fry over high heat for 3–5 minutes, until evenly browned. Add the sesame seeds and stir-fry for about 1 minute, until golden, then remove from the heat.

Remove the bouquet garni and lemon grass from the soup and discard. Ladle the soup and vegetables into a warm tureen, add the pork and sesame seeds, and garnish with a dash of sesame oil and some cilantro leaves. Serve immediately.

A piggy party

Rack of pork with ginger cooked in a salt crust

PREPARATION TIME: 30 MINUTES
MARINATING TIME: 24 HOURS
COOKING TIME: 1½ HOURS

SERVES 6

3½ ounces fresh ginger root
6 garlic cloves
1 bunch of fresh parsley
3 tablespoons olive oil
1 rack of 6 pork chops
13½ cups coarse sea salt

Put the ginger, garlic, parsley, and olive oil in a food processor and process until finely chopped and thoroughly combined.

Make small incisions in the rack at the ribs. Spread the ginger paste over the rack, wrap it in plastic wrap, and let marinate in the refrigerator for 24 hours.

The next day, preheat the oven to 325°F. Spread a layer of coarse salt in an ovenproof dish, place the rack on top and cover completely with more coarse salt. You can dampen the salt slightly to make it easier to shape. Bake for 1½ hours.

Break the salt crust and place the rack on a carving board to serve.

casserole of Rack of pork in hay

PREPARATION TIME: 15 MINUTES
COOKING TIME: 1¼ HOURS

SERVES 6

1 rack of 6 pork chops, trimmed
6 garlic cloves, green shoots removed, cut into thin sticks
4 tablespoons olive oil
3 handfuls of untreated hay
1 fresh thyme sprig
¾ cup white wine
2 shallots
6 Jerusalem artichokes

Preheat the oven to 350°F. Make small incisions in the rack with a sharp knife. Insert the sticks of garlic into the slits.

Heat the oil in a skillet. Add the rack and cook over high heat, turning occasionally, for about 10 minutes, until evenly browned.

Put the hay and thyme in a casserole and pour in the white wine. Place the rack, whole shallots, and Jerusalem artichokes on top and cover with the lid. Cook in the oven for 1 hour. Serve straight from the casserole.

A REMINISCENCE

This recipe has something special about it because it takes me back to the end of summer, during the vacation, when the whole countryside was scented with dried grass ... You are welcome to adapt it using a type of hay redolent of your past, from a farm you knew in a place you loved. And let the magic weave its spell. I myself use the hay at Gué from Marie-Cécile and Marcelou: come and smell it and you will understand why!

Pork tenderloins with porcini stuffing

PREPARATION TIME: 45 MINUTES
COOKING TIME: 20 MINUTES

SERVES 6

3 small pork tenderloins, total weight about 2½ pounds
4 garlic cloves
1 bunch of fresh parsley
7 ounces porcini mushrooms, chopped, plus 6 whole
  large porcini mushrooms
¼ cup sweet butter
18 thin slices of smoked bacon
salt and pepper

Using a small, sharp knife, cut round the tenderloins in a spiral to open them up like snails. Season with salt and pepper.

Chop the garlic with the parsley. Combine the chopped mushrooms with half the garlic and parsley mixture. Melt half the butter in a skillet, add the chopped mushroom mixture, and cook over medium-low heat, stirring occasionally, for about 5 minutes.

Spread each piece of pork with the mushroom stuffing, roll up, and wrap each one in 6 slices of bacon. Place them in a heavy pan and cook, turning frequently, for 15 minutes.

Melt the remaining butter in another pan. Add the large whole porcinis and the remaining garlic and parsley mixture and cook, turning occasionally, for about 8 minutes. Cut each pork packet into six and serve with the whole mushrooms and the garlic and parsley butter.

tenderloins in a fresh herb crust

PREPARATION TIME: 20 MINUTES
CHILLING TIME: 1 HOUR
COOKING TIME: 15 MINUTES

SERVES 6

2 eggplants, cut into large batons
2 zucchini, cut into large batons
11 ounces cherry tomatoes
6 tablespoons olive oil
3 small pork tenderloins, total weight about 2½ pounds

FOR THE HERB CRUST

⅔ cup sweet butter
1¾ cups white bread crumbs
2 fresh tarragon sprigs
2 fresh basil sprigs
2 fresh chervil sprigs
1 shallot, chopped
salt and pepper

First make the herb crust. Beat the butter in a bowl until creamy, then beat in the bread crumbs, tarragon leaves, basil leaves, chervil leaves, and shallot. Season with salt and pepper. Spread out the mixture between two sheets of wax or parchment paper and chill in the refrigerator for at least 1 hour before using.

Toss the eggplants, zucchini, and tomatoes in half the olive oil. Heat a ridged griddle pan, add the vegetables, and cook over low heat, turning occasionally, until tender but still firm.

Meanwhile, heat the remaining oil in a skillet. Add the tenderloins and cook over high heat for about 2 minutes on each side, until browned, then lower the heat and cook, turning occasionally, for 7–8 minutes, until cooked through and tender. Preheat the broiler.

Transfer the pork to the pan of vegetables. Place a strip of herb crust on top of each tenderloin and broil until the crust is lightly browned. Serve immediately.

If necessary, wrap the handle of the griddle pan in foil before broiling to protect it from damage.

a piggy party

Pork with dates and dried apricots

PREPARATION TIME: 10 MINUTES
COOKING TIME: 1 HOUR

SERVES 6

2½ pounds boneless Boston butt
6 tablespoons olive oil
14 ounces onions, sliced
1 teaspoon ground ginger
1 teaspoon ground cinnamon
1 teaspoon ground cumin
½ teaspoon saffron threads
5 ounces dried dates
5 ounces dried apricots
6 garlic cloves, unpeeled

Preheat the oven to 325°F. Cut the pork into even-size pieces. Heat the olive oil in a large, flameproof casserole. Add the pork, onions, ginger, cinnamon, cumin, and saffron and cook over low heat, stirring occasionally, for 10 minutes, until the onions have softened and meat is evenly browned.

Add the dates, apricots and garlic and pour in ¾ cup water. Cover and cook in the oven for 1 hour, checking frequently and adding more water if the casserole seems to be drying out.

Pork and citrus fruit with ratatouille

PREPARATION TIME: 45 MINUTES
MARINATING TIME: 2 HOURS
COOKING TIME: 1¼ HOURS

SERVES 6

2¼ pounds boneless pork loin
grated rind and juice of 3 oranges
juice of 1 grapefruit
7 tablespoons olive oil
4 onions, sliced
4 garlic cloves, crushed
3 zucchini, diced
3 eggplants, diced
6 tomatoes, diced
2 bay leaves
1 fresh thyme sprig

Put the pork in a nonmetallic dish. Sprinkle with the orange rind and pour the orange and grapefruit juice over it. Let marinate in a cool place for 2 hours.

Preheat the oven to 350°F.

Heat 5 tablespoons of the olive oil in a large, flameproof casserole. Add the onions, garlic, zucchini, eggplants, and tomatoes and cook over low heat, stirring occasionally, for 8–10 minutes, until softened. Add the bay leaves and thyme and cook in the oven, uncovered, for 1 hour, stirring frequently.

Drain the pork, reserving the marinade. Heat the remaining olive oil in a skillet. Add the pork and cook over high heat, turning frequently, for about 10 minutes, until evenly browned. Transfer to an ovenproof dish and pour in the reserved marinade. Place in the oven and cook, basting frequently, for 1 hour.

Transfer the pork to a plate. Mix the ratatouille with the roasting juices, then place the pork on top. Return to the oven and cook for a further 15 minutes. Remove and slice the pork, then serve it on a bed of ratatouille.

a piggy party

Pot roast confit with lemon-flavored cilantro salad

PREPARATION TIME: 20 MINUTES
COOKING TIME: 4 HOURS

SERVES 6

2 garlic cloves, crushed
1 teaspoon coarse sea salt
1 teaspoon coarsely ground black pepper
1 teaspoon ground coriander
1 boneless Boston butt, weighing about 2½ pounds
2¼ pounds goose or duck fat
2 bay leaves
2 bunches of fresh cilantro
juice of 1 lemon
2 tablespoons olive oil
1 pink grapefruit
1 preserved lemon, chopped (available from
  gourmet grocers or Middle Eastern stores)

Combine the garlic, salt, pepper, and ground coriander in a bowl and rub the spice mixture all over the meat.

Melt the goose fat in a large, flameproof casserole. Add the pork and bay leaves and cook over low heat for 3–4 hours. Remove the pork from the casserole and set aside, with a little fat around it, wrapped in plastic wrap.

Pull off the leaves from the cilantro stems and place in a bowl. Combine the lemon juice and olive oil in a pitcher, pour the dressing over the cilantro, and toss lightly.

Peel the grapefruit, removing all traces of pith, and cut into segments. Discard the membranes. Coarsely chop the segments. Unwrap the pork, slice it and serve garnished with the grapefruit, preserved lemon, and cilantro salad.

A piggy party

Pig's cheek with fennel and olives

PREPARATION TIME: 45 MINUTES
COOKING TIME: 1 HOUR

SERVES 6

½ cup olive oil, plus extra for drizzling
18 pig's cheeks (meat only), to be ordered from your butcher
¾ cup white wine
4 garlic cloves
1 bunch of fresh curly parsley
scant 1 cup pitted black Greek olives
6 ripe tomatoes
4 fennel bulbs, cut into fourths
1 bunch of fresh flat-leaf parsley

Heat the olive oil in a flameproof casserole. Add the pig's cheeks and cook over high heat, turning frequently, for 10 minutes, until browned all over. Pour in the white wine, lower the heat, cover, and simmer for 1 hour, until tender.

Preheat the oven to 325°F.

Chop 2 of the garlic cloves with the curly parsley and 2 cloves with the olives. Cut out an opening at the stalk end of the tomatoes and stuff them with the garlic and parsley mixture and half the olive mixture. Place in an ovenproof dish, drizzle with olive oil, and bake in the oven for 20 minutes.

Cook the fennel in salted boiling water for 15 minutes.

When the cheeks are tender, add the fennel and the remaining olive mixture.

Divide the pig's cheeks, fennel, and olive mixture among six individual plates. Add a tomato to each and garnish with flat-leaf parsley.

a piggy party

My ham and pasta shells

PREPARATION TIME: 10 MINUTES
COOKING TIME: 10 MINUTES

SERVES 6

4½ cups pasta shells
generous ½ cup fresh pork belly, cut into matchsticks
2 garlic cloves, crushed
scant ½ cup white wine
1 cup heavy cream
6 slices of good-quality jambon de Paris or other
  unsmoked, fully-cooked ham, cut into strips
3½ ounces Parmesan cheese, shaved
6 egg yolks
salt

Cook the pasta shells in a large pan of salted boiling water for about 10 minutes, until tender but still firm to the bite.

Meanwhile, cook the pork belly and garlic in a heavy pan over medium–low heat, until golden brown. Stir in the white wine, scraping up any sediment from the base of the pan. Stir in the cream and cook, stirring constantly, until slightly thickened.

Drain the pasta shells and toss in the cream, pork belly, and garlic sauce. Spoon a mound of pasta shells on to each of six serving plates, divide the ham strips and Parmesan shavings among them, and top with an egg yolk.

Crisp tenderloins with carrots

PREPARATION TIME: 30 MINUTES
COOKING TIME: 30 MINUTES

SERVES 6

⅔ cup olive oil
3 small pork tenderloins, total weight about 2½ pounds
6 large potatoes, grated
1 bunch of fresh chives, chopped
6 eggs, lightly beaten
24 baby carrots, preferably with tops still attached
scant 1 cup chicken stock
¼ cup sweet butter
1 tablespoon brown sugar
1 bunch of fresh parsley, chopped

Heat 4 tablespoons of the olive oil in a skillet. Add the pork and cook over high heat, turning frequently, for about 10 minutes, until evenly browned. Remove the pan from the heat.

Combine the grated potatoes, chives, and eggs in a bowl. Roll each of the tenderloins with one-third of the potato mixture in plastic wrap, sealing the packets securely. Cook them in a pan of boiling water for 10 minutes.

Put the carrots in a flameproof casserole, placing them side by side in a single layer. Add enough of the chicken stock to cover them to a depth of ½ inch. Add the butter and sugar. Cook over low heat, turning frequently, for 20 minutes, until the carrots are tender and the sauce is syrupy.

Lift the tenderloins out of the water with a slotted spoon and remove and discard the plastic wrap. Heat 4 tablespoons of the remaining olive oil in a pan, add the tenderloins, and cook over medium heat, turning frequently, until golden and crisp. Remove from the pan and drain on paper towels.

Mix the parsley with the remaining olive oil. Make a bed of glazed carrots on each of six serving plates. Cut the tenderloins in half and add to the plates, then sprinkle with the parsley oil, and serve.

Pork medallions with bacon

PREPARATION TIME: 20 MINUTES
COOKING TIME: 1 HOUR

SERVES 6

18 garlic cloves
8–10 tablespoons olive oil
3 eggplants, cut lengthwise into batons
12 thin, center-cut, boneless pork chops
6 slices of speck or prosciutto
¾ cup white wine
¼ cup sweet butter, chilled
salt and pepper

Place the whole garlic in a pan and cover with half the olive oil. Cook over very low heat for about 40 minutes, until the garlic is tender. Remove the pan from the heat and set aside to cool, then remove the garlic with a slotted spoon, and set aside. Reserve the garlic-flavored oil.

Heat the garlic-flavored oil in a skillet. Add the eggplants and cook, turning occasionally, until golden brown and tender.

Meanwhile, heat the remaining olive oil in another pan. Add the pork and speck or prosciutto and cook over high heat, turning occasionally, for about 5 minutes, until the pork is evenly browned. Add the white wine, bring to a boil, and cook until reduced. Add half the butter and cook for a further 5 minutes, then season with salt and pepper.

Place two pork chops and a slice of speck or prosciutto on each of six plates. Divide the eggplants and garlic among them. Add the remaining butter to the meat juice and whisk over low heat until glossy, then spoon over the meat, and serve.

Millefeuilles of pork and artichokes

PREPARATION TIME: 20 MINUTES
COOKING TIME: 15 MINUTES

SERVES 6

24 fresh sage leaves
scant ½ cup sunflower oil
4 sheets of filo pastry
1 egg, lightly beaten
6 artichoke hearts, thawed if frozen
12 thin, center-cut, boneless pork chops
salt

Blanch 12 of the sage leaves in a pan of salted boiling water for 10 seconds, then drain, and pat dry. Place them in a bowl, add the sunflower oil, and set aside.

Brush both sides of the filo pastry sheets with the beaten egg. Divide the remaining sage leaves between two of them and cover each with the remaining filo sheets. Cut each filo galette into 12.

Halve each artichoke heart horizontally. Heat the sage-flavored oil in a skillet. Add the pork and artichoke hearts and cook, turning occasionally, for about 6 minutes, until the pork is golden and cooked through and the artichoke hearts are tender but still firm to the bite. Remove from the pan and keep warm. Add the filo galettes to the pan and cook, turning once, for about 2 minutes.

Make alternate layers of filo galette, artichoke heart, and pork on individual serving plates and pour the sage oil over them.

A piggy party

My stuffed vegetables

POTATOES

PREPARATION TIME: 20 MINUTES
COOKING TIME: 45 MINUTES

SERVES 6

12 waxy potatoes
scant 1 cup, chopped smoked bacon
5 ounces bulk (breakfast) sausages, skins removed
2 fresh thyme sprigs, chopped
2¼ cups diced cooked roast pork
¾ cup cooked lentils
1 bunch of fresh tarragon, chopped
walnut oil, for drizzling
salt and pepper

Preheat the oven to 300°F. Parboil the potatoes for 15 minutes, then drain. Meanwhile, cook the bacon and sausagemeat in a heavy skillet for 10 minutes, until evenly browned. Sprinkle with the thyme and mix with the cooked roast pork and lentils in a bowl. Stir in the tarragon and season.

Cut off and reserve the tops of the potatoes and scoop out the flesh. Fill the cavities with the pork stuffing, replace the tops, place in an ovenproof dish, and drizzle with walnut oil. Bake in the oven, basting frequently, for 30 minutes.

TOMATOES

PREPARATION TIME: 20 MINUTES
COOKING TIME: 25 MINUTES

SERVES 6

2 slices of country-style white bread, crusts removed
scant ½ cup crème fraîche
2 tablespoons olive oil
2 garlic cloves, chopped
1 teaspoon chopped fresh ginger root
8 firm tomatoes
3⅔ cups diced cooked roast pork
1 bunch of fresh basil, chopped
2 eggs, lightly beaten
salt and pepper

Preheat the oven to 300°F. Tear the bread into pieces and soak in the crème fraîche. Heat the oil in a skillet, add the garlic and ginger and cook for 2 minutes, then remove from the heat.

Finely dice 2 of the tomatoes and squeeze out any excess liquid from the bread. Combine the pork, bread, basil, and eggs and season. Stir in the diced tomatoes and the garlic and ginger. Cut off and reserve the tops of the remaining tomatoes and scoop out the flesh. Fill them with the pork stuffing, replace the tops, and place in an ovenproof dish. Bake, basting frequently with the cooking juices, for 20 minutes.

ONIONS

PREPARATION TIME: 20 MINUTES
COOKING TIME: 3½ HOURS

SERVES 6

6 large onions
2 tablespoons olive oil, plus extra for drizzling
1 teaspoon ground cinnamon
1 teaspoon curry powder
7 ounces bulk (breakfast) sausages, skins removed
2¼ cups diced cooked roast pork
1 teaspoon pine nuts, toasted
1 bunch of fresh mint, chopped

Preheat the oven to 250°F. Place each onion on a piece of foil, drizzle with olive oil, fold up the foil to enclose the onions, and bake for 3 hours.

Mix the spices with the sausagemeat. Heat the oil in a skillet, add the sausagemeat and pork, and cook, stirring frequently, for about 10 minutes, until evenly browned. Stir in the pine nuts and mint and remove from the heat.

Remove the onions from the oven and increase the temperature to 300°F. Unwrap the onions. Cut off the tops and reserve, then scoop out the flesh. Mix the onion flesh with the stuffing and fill each onion. Replace the tops, place in an ovenproof dish, and bake for 30 minutes.

Pork tenderloins with tomato

PREPARATION TIME: 20 MINUTES
COOKING TIME: 3 HOURS

SERVES 6

12 tomatoes, halved and seeded
5 tablespoons olive oil, plus extra for drizzling
6 large shallots
1 bunch of fresh parsley, chopped
1 garlic clove, chopped
3 small pork tenderloins, total weight about 2½ pounds
sea salt

Preheat the oven to 225°F. Cut 24 sheets of wax or parchment paper each large enough to enclose a tomato half. Place a tomato half on each sheet, drizzle with olive oil, and sprinkle with sea salt. Fold up the paper to enclose the tomato halves and bake for 3 hours.

Put the shallots in an ovenproof dish, drizzle with olive oil, and cook in the oven with the tomatoes for 1 hour, until softened. Mix the parsley and garlic with 1 tablespoon of the olive oil in a bowl. Cut the pork tenderloins into six. Heat the remaining olive oil in a pan, add the tenderloins, and cook over medium heat, turning occasionally, for 15—20 minutes, until evenly browned and cooked through. Add the parsley and garlic mixture.

Unwrap the tomatoes and divide them among individual plates with the pork and shallots. Drizzle with the garlic-flavored pan juices and serve.

A piggy party

Boston butt cooked in beer

PREPARATION TIME: 10 MINUTES
COOKING TIME: 1¾ HOURS

SERVES 6

2 tablespoons olive oil
1 piece of boneless Boston butt, weighing about 2½ pounds
3 shallots, sliced
3 garlic cloves, finely chopped
2 bay leaves
generous ½ cup chopped smoked bacon
2¼ cups brown ale beer
11 ounces spätzle or fresh pasta
¼ cup sweet butter
salt

Heat the oil in a large, flameproof casserole. Add the pork and cook over high heat, turning frequently, for about 10 minutes, until evenly browned. Add the shallots, garlic, bay leaves, and bacon, lower the heat, and cook, stirring occasionally, for 10 minutes until beginning to color. Stir in the beer, scraping up the sediment from the base of the casserole with a wooden spoon, and bring to a boil. Cover and simmer over low heat, basting frequently, for 1¼ hours. Preheat the oven to 350°F.

Transfer the pork to a roasting pan, baste with the cooking juices, and place in the oven. Cook, basting frequently, for 15 minutes, until glazed.

Cook the spätzle or pasta in a large pan of salted boiling water until tender, then remove with a slotted spoon or drain. (The spätzle will be cooked when they rise to the surface and fresh pasta will take 2–3 minutes. Alternatively, follow the instructions on the packet.) Stir in the butter, and when that has melted, stir in the garlic, shallots, and bacon together with the remaining cooking juices.

Serve the pork with the spätzle or pasta mixture.

Curry

PREPARATION TIME: 30 MINUTES
COOKING TIME: 1 HOUR 35 MINUTES

SERVES 6

4 tablespoons olive oil
2½ pounds boneless Boston butt, cut into cubes
3 onions, sliced
2 tablespoons curry powder
1 teaspoon ground coriander
scant 1 cup white wine
scant 1 cup heavy cream
scant 1 cup coconut milk
3½ ounces Granny Smith or other tart eating apples
3½ ounces bananas
3½ ounces pineapple, cut into cubes
scant 1 cup shelled almonds
1 bunch of fresh cilantro, chopped

Heat the olive oil in a large, flameproof casserole. Add the pork and onions and cook over medium heat, stirring frequently, for 8–10 minutes, until the pork is evenly browned and the onions have softened. Add the curry powder and ground coriander and cook, stirring constantly, for 2 minutes.

Stir in the white wine, scraping up any sediment from the base of the casserole with a wooden spoon, and bring to a boil. Lower the heat, cover, and simmer for 45 minutes.

Stir in the cream and cook for 15 minutes, until reduced. Add half the coconut milk and simmer for a further 15 minutes. Peel and core the apples and cut into cubes. Cut the bananas into chunks. Add the apples, bananas, pineapple, and almonds to the casserole and simmer for a further 5 minutes.

Swirl in the remaining coconut milk, sprinkle with the fresh cilantro, and serve.

 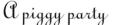

tenderloins with peanuts

PREPARATION TIME: 10 MINUTES
COOKING TIME: 30 MINUTES

SERVES 6

3 green bell peppers
3 yellow bell peppers
1 bunch of fresh cilantro
2 tablespoons curry paste
2 garlic cloves, crushed
scant 1 cup peanuts, chopped
scant 1 cup coconut milk
4 tablespoons peanut oil
3 small pork tenderloins, total weight about 2½ pounds

Preheat the oven to 350°F. Place the whole bell peppers on a cookie sheet and roast, turning occasionally, for 20 minutes, until the skins are charred. Remove from the oven and let cool. Peel off the skins and set the whole bell peppers aside.

Chop the stems and leaves of the cilantro, then mix with the curry paste, garlic, and peanuts in a bowl. Alternatively, place the bunch of cilantro, the curry paste, and garlic in a food processor and process until finely chopped and thoroughly combined. Dry-fry this paste in a pan, stirring constantly, until it gives off its aroma. Stir in the coconut milk and cook until reduced.

Heat the oil in a skillet. Add the tenderloins and cook over high heat, turning occasionally, for 10 minutes, until evenly browned and cooked through. Meanwhile, reheat the bell peppers in the oven at 350°F.

Arrange the tenderloins and the whole peppers on a board and serve the sauce separately.

Blanquette of pork

PREPARATION TIME: 45 MINUTES
COOKING TIME: 1¼ HOURS

SERVES 6

1 onion
2 cloves
4 tablespoons olive oil
2½ pounds boneless Boston butt, cut into large cubes
1 tablespoon all-purpose flour
2 tablespoons chicken bouillon powder
1 bouquet garni
6 waxy potatoes, diced
3 carrots, sliced
1¾ cups shelled baby peas
1½ cups shelled fava beans
1¼ cups heavy cream
juice of 1 lemon

Stud the onion with the cloves and set aside. Heat the olive oil in a pan. Add the pork and cook over high heat, stirring frequently, for about 10 minutes, until evenly browned. Lower the heat, stir in the flour, and cook, stirring constantly, for 5 minutes.

Pour in enough water to cover the meat by twice its depth and add the chicken bouillon powder, the bouquet garni, and the onion studded with cloves. Simmer, skimming the surface frequently, for 1 hour.

Meanwhile, cook the potatoes, carrots, peas, and beans in salted boiling water until tender but still firm to the bite. Drain well.

Remove the meat from the pan with a slotted spoon. Stir the cream into the cooking liquid and cook, stirring occasionally, until reduced and smooth. Return the meat to the pan, add the vegetables, and reheat. Stir in the lemon juice and serve.

BLANQUETTE

Blanquette is rich creamy stew, usually made with white meats. The meat is cooked without initial browning, and the sauce is thickened with roux and enriched with cream. Blanquette derives from the French word blanc (white).

Rack of pork with pepper and pissaladière

PREPARATION TIME: 45 MINUTES
COOKING TIME: 2 HOURS

SERVES 6

6 tablespoons olive oil
1 rack of 6 pork chops
6 onions, sliced
1 fresh rosemary sprig, chopped
2 fresh thyme sprigs, chopped
7 ounces bread dough (available from pasta and
  pizza shops and some grocers)
all-purpose flour, for dusting
12 salted anchovies
20 Greek olives
scant 1 cup white wine
1 small can or jar of green peppercorns
scant 1 cup heavy cream

Preheat the oven to 325°F. Heat 4 tablespoons of the oil in a roasting pan. Add the rack of pork and cook over high heat, turning frequently, for about 10 minutes, until evenly browned. Transfer the pan to the oven and roast, basting frequently, for 1¼ hours.

Heat the remaining oil in a skillet. Add the onions, rosemary, and thyme and cook over low heat, stirring occasionally, until softened but not colored. Remove the skillet from the heat.

Roll out the bread dough on a lightly floured surface to a round like a pizza and place on a cookie sheet. Cover it with the cooked onions, the anchovies, and half of the olives. Leave in a warm place to rise for 30 minutes.

Remove the pork from the oven, cover with foil and let stand while the pissaladière is baking. Increase the oven temperature to 400°F. Bake the pissaladière for 15 minutes.

Transfer the pork to a carving board. Set the roasting pan over high heat and stir in the white wine, scraping up any sediment from the base of the pan. Add the green peppercorns and the remaining olives, bring to a boil, and cook until reduced. Stir in the cream and cook for a further 5 minutes, but do not let the sauce boil.

Carve the rack, place the chops on a serving dish, and spoon the sauce over them. Serve with the pissaladière.

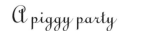

tenderloins with sauerkraut

PREPARATION TIME: 15 MINUTES
COOKING TIME: 25 MINUTES

SERVES 6

2¼ pounds ready-made sauerkraut
¾ cup Riesling wine or other dry white wine
4 tablespoons olive oil
3 small pork tenderloins, total weight about 2½ pounds
4 shallots, sliced
10 juniper berries, crushed
3 tablespoons cognac or brandy
scant ½ cup crème fraîche
1 bunch of fresh chives, chopped

Place the sauerkraut in a pan, add half the wine, and cook over low heat.

Heat the olive oil in a skillet. Add the pork and cook over high heat, turning occasionally, for about 10 minutes, until evenly browned and cooked through. Remove from the pan, set aside, and keep warm.

Add the shallots and juniper berries to the same pan and cook over low heat, stirring occasionally, for about 5 minutes, until softened. Add the cognac or brandy, heat for a few seconds, then ignite. When the flames have died down, add the remaining wine, and simmer for 5 minutes. Stir in the crème fraîche and cook for a further 5 minutes.

Divide the sauerkraut among six individual plates. Slice the pork, add to the plates, and top with the shallot and juniper cream. Garnish with the chives and serve.

Pork chops with artichokes and new potatoes

PREPARATION TIME: 30 MINUTES
COOKING TIME: 20 MINUTES

SERVES 6

12 poivrade artichokes or purple artichokes
1¾ pounds small new potatoes
5 tablespoons olive oil
2 garlic cloves, coarsely chopped
4 fresh parsley sprigs, coarsely chopped
¼ cup sweet butter
6 center-cut, boneless pork loin chops
salt and pepper

Prepare the artichokes by peeling the stalks and removing the outer leaves. Cut off the tops of the leaves with kitchen scissors, then cut each artichoke lengthwise, and remove the hairy choke.

Parboil the potatoes in salted water for 5 minutes, then drain.

Heat the olive oil in a skillet. Add the artichokes and cook over low heat, turning occasionally, until golden brown and tender. Remove from the skillet and keep warm. Add the potatoes to the skillet and cook, stirring occasionally, until golden brown all over. Stir in the garlic and parsley.

Meanwhile, melt the butter in another skillet. Add the chops and cook over medium heat for 5 minutes on each side, or until golden brown and cooked through. Season with salt and pepper.

Divide the chops, artichokes, and potatoes among six individual plates, spoon the garlic and parsley cooking juices over them, and serve.

A piggy party

Pork chops with Saint-Marcellin cheese

PREPARATION TIME: 20 MINUTES
COOKING TIME: 25 MINUTES

SERVES 6

3½ cups short macaroni
1½ tablespoons sweet butter
3 tablespoons all-purpose flour
2¼ cups fresh whole milk
a pinch of freshly grated nutmeg
3½ ounces Vieux Comté or Gruyère cheese, diced
scant 1 cup grated Swiss cheese
6 pork loin chops
olive oil, for brushing
3 sharp Saint-Marcellin or other soft goats' cheeses,
   such as Banon, halved
salt and pepper

Preheat the oven to 325°F. Cook the macaroni in salted boiling water for 8–10 minutes, until tender but still firm to the bite, then drain. Melt the butter in a pan, stir in the flour, and cook, stirring constantly, for 2 minutes. Gradually stir in the milk, add the nutmeg, and cook, stirring constantly, for 8 minutes.

Preheat the broiler. Combine the Vieux Comté and macaroni and place in an ovenproof dish. Pour the sauce over the top and sprinkle with the grated Swiss cheese. Bake in the oven for 10 minutes, then season with salt and pepper.

Meanwhile, brush the chops with oil and cook under the broiler for 5 minutes on each side, or until well browned and cooked through. Place half a Saint-Marcellin cheese on each of the chops and broil until the cheese melts.

Place a cheese-covered chop on each of six individual plates, divide the macaroni among them, and serve.

a piggy party

tenderloins with maple syrup

PREPARATION TIME: 15 MINUTES
COOKING TIME: 25 MINUTES

SERVES 6

6 rhubarb sticks, cut into short lengths
1 tablespoon brown sugar
1½ tablespoons sweet butter
3 small pork tenderloins, total weight about 2½ pounds
3 tablespoons white port
2 tablespoons maple syrup
1 teaspoon ground ginger
½ cup hazelnuts, crushed
sea salt and coarsely ground black pepper

Put the rhubarb in a pan, add 2 tablespoons water, and cook over low heat for 5 minutes. Add the sugar and 1½ teaspoons of the butter, and cook for a further 5 minutes, until the rhubarb is soft.

Heat the remaining butter in a skillet. Add the pork and cook over high heat, turning occasionally, for about 10 minutes, until golden brown and cooked through. Add the port and maple syrup and cook, basting the meat frequently, until the sauce has reduced to a syrupy texture.

Slice the pork tenderloins. Stir the ginger into the rhubarb, season with sea salt and coarsely ground black pepper, add the crushed hazelnuts, and serve with the pork.

tenderloins with pesto and crunchy vegetable salad

PREPARATION TIME: 20 MINUTES
COOKING TIME: 15 MINUTES

SERVES 6

1 bunch of fresh basil
3 tablespoons pine nuts
1 garlic clove, chopped
⅔ cup Parmesan cheese shavings
1¼ cups olive oil
2 carrots
2 zucchini
2 cucumbers
3 celery stalks
1 red onion, thinly sliced
1 tablespoon balsamic vinegar
3 small pork tenderloins, total weight about 2½ pounds
sea salt

To make the pesto, put the basil, pine nuts and garlic in a mortar and crush to a paste with a pestle, then work in the Parmesan. Gradually add scant 1 cup of the olive oil, mixing well with a wooden spoon.

Using a vegetable peeler, cut the carrots, zucchini, cucumber, and celery into thin strips, then slice the strips lengthwise into narrow ribbons. Place the vegetable ribbons in a bowl, add the onion, and mix well. Whisk together 4 tablespoons of the remaining olive oil and the balsamic vinegar in a pitcher, season with sea salt, and add to the vegetables.

Heat the remaining olive oil in a skillet. Add the tenderloins and cook over high heat, turning occasionally, for 15 minutes, until well browned and cooked through.

Slice the tenderloins, place on individual serving plates, and spoon the pesto over them. Divide the vegetable salad among the plates and serve immediately. This dish can also be served cold.

tenderloins in sweet-and-sour sauce

PREPARATION TIME: 20 MINUTES
COOKING TIME: 15 MINUTES

SERVES 6

1 bunch of green asparagus
4 tablespoons sunflower oil
3 small pork tenderloins, thinly sliced
1 cucumber, thinly sliced
2 zucchini, thinly sliced
1 red bell pepper, seeded and thinly sliced
1 yellow bell pepper, seeded and thinly sliced
1 red onion, thinly sliced
1 bunch of fresh chives, cut into ½-inch lengths

FOR THE SWEET-AND-SOUR SAUCE

1 red onion, chopped
2 garlic cloves, chopped
¼ cup sugar
2 ounces canned pineapple, drained
1 tablespoon tomato ketchup
1 tablespoon wine vinegar

First make the sweet-and-sour sauce. Combine all the ingredients in a pan and cook over low heat for 5 minutes. Set aside.

Cut the asparagus into pieces and slice lengthwise. Heat the sunflower oil in a wok or large skillet. Add the pork and stir-fry over high heat for about 5 minutes, until evenly browned. Add the asparagus, cucumber, zucchini, bell peppers, and onion and stir-fry for 5 minutes, until tender but still crisp. Add the sweet-and-sour sauce and cook, stirring constantly, for a further 2 minutes.

Sprinkle with chives and serve immediately.

a piggy party

Tagliatelle with bacon

PREPARATION TIME: 20 MINUTES
COOKING TIME: 10 MINUTES

SERVES 6

scant 1 cup chopped fresh pork belly
scant 1 cup chopped smoked bacon
5 ounces Spanish chorizo sausage (see pages 68 and 69),
  cut into batons, or smoked Mexican–American style chorizo
  (see *Sources*), cooked, drained, and cut into pieces
2 garlic cloves, sliced
1 pound 5 ounces fresh tagliatelle
1 bunch of fresh basil, finely chopped
sea salt

Heat a nonstick skillet. Add the fresh pork belly, bacon, and Spanish chorizo, and cook over medium heat, stirring frequently, for 5 minutes. (If using Mexican–American chorizo, do not add it yet.) Add the garlic and cook, stirring frequently, for a few minutes more, until golden brown.

Meanwhile, cook the tagliatelle in a large pan of salted boiling water for 2–3 minutes, until tender but still firm to the bite. Alternatively, cook according to the packet instructions.

Drain the pasta, add it (and the Mexican–American chorizo if using) to the pan with the pork, bacon, and garlic, and toss well. Add the basil, season with sea salt, and serve.

A piggy party

Roast pork loin with cider vinegar on a bed of sweet potatoes

PREPARATION TIME: 20 MINUTES
COOKING TIME: 1½ HOURS

SERVES 6

6 tablespoons olive oil
2¼ pounds center-cut, boneless pork loin, trimmed of fat
1 eggplant, cut into large cubes
2 tomatoes, cut into large cubes
2 zucchini, cut into large cubes
2 garlic cloves, chopped
2 onions, chopped
scant 1 cup hard cider
¼ cup sweet butter, cut into pieces
1 pound 5 ounces sweet potatoes
⅔ cup cider vinegar
2 tablespoons sugar
fresh flat-leaf parsley and fresh cilantro leaves, to garnish

Preheat the oven to 325°F. Heat the olive oil in a large, flameproof casserole. Add the pork and cook over high heat, turning occasionally, for about 10 minutes, until evenly browned.

Lower the heat, add the eggplant, tomatoes, zucchini, garlic, and onions, and cook, stirring occasionally, for 5 minutes. Pour in the hard cider and bring to a boil. Cover and cook in the oven for 1 hour. Add the butter, return the casserole to the oven, and cook for a further 15 minutes.

Meanwhile, cook the sweet potatoes in salted boiling water for about 20 minutes, until tender. Drain and mash coarsely with a fork. Keep warm.

Combine the cider vinegar and sugar in a pan. Cook over low heat, stirring until the sugar has dissolved, then continue to cook until reduced and syrupy.

Make a bed of sweet potato on each of six serving plates. Slice the pork. Divide the meat and vegetables, with their cooking juices, among the plates. Spoon a little vinegar syrup over each serving and garnish with parsley and cilantro leaves.

a piggy party

Wild boar

Wild boar terrine

PREPARATION TIME: 45 MINUTES
MARINATING TIME: 4 HOURS
COOKING TIME: 3 HOURS

MAKES 7 × 1 PINT JARS

1 pound 5 ounces boneless arm shoulder of wild boar
  (or 2½ pounds boneless picnic ham)
1 pound fresh pork belly
¼ cup red port
scant ½ cup red wine
2 tablespoons Armagnac
8 juniper berries, crushed
1 teaspoon Quatre-épices (see page 154)
14 ounces picnic ham (if using wild boar)
5 ounces pig's liver
2 shallots, chopped
2 garlic cloves, chopped
1 tablespoon salt
1 teaspoon fresh thyme
pepper

Cut 7 ounces of the wild boar into small cubes and place in a dish. Cut a generous half-cup of the fresh pork belly into matchsticks and add them, the port, the red wine, the Armagnac, juniper berries, and spice, mix well, and let marinate for 4 hours.

Coarsely grind the remaining wild boar and/or picnic ham, the remaining pork belly and the liver. Combine the ground meat, shallots, garlic, salt, thyme, and a pinch of pepper in a large bowl. Add the cubed wild boar and the pork belly matchsticks, together with the marinade, and mix well.

Sterilize seven wide-mouthed 1-pint jars and their lids. Fill the jars with the mixture, pressing it down well, and seal. Place the jars in canning kettle, add water to cover, and simmer for 3 hours.

Remove the jars from the kettle and let cool, then store in a dry place for several days before serving.

Marcassin pâté

PREPARATION TIME: 45 MINUTES
MARINATING TIME: 24 HOURS
COOKING TIME: 2 HOURS

MAKES 3¼ POUNDS

2¼ pounds boneless arm shoulder of marcassin
  (wild boar under the age of 6 months) (or domestic Boston butt)
3½ ounces sliced smoked bacon
2 onions
4 cloves
2¼ cups Côtes du Rhône or Shiraz wine
2 carrots, diced
3 bay leaves
1 fresh thyme sprig
14 ounces smoked boneless picnic ham

4 teaspoons salt
2 tablespoons sweet butter
4 shallots, thinly sliced
4 garlic cloves, thinly sliced
1 tablespoon cornstarch
scant 1 cup heavy cream
4 eggs, lightly beaten
3 tablespoons dark rum
pork fat or lard, for greasing

Cut half the wild boar into thin strips and place it and all the bacon in a dish. Stud the onions with the cloves, add to the dish with the red wine, carrots, bay leaves, and thyme, and let marinate for 24 hours.

Preheat the oven to 250°F. Coarsely grind the remaining wild boar and the picnic ham, mix together in a bowl, and add the salt. Melt the butter in a skillet. Add the shallots and garlic and cook over low heat, stirring occasionally, for 5 minutes, until softened. Stir the shallots and garlic into the meat mixture.

Remove the bay leaves and thyme from the marinade and reserve. Remove the strips of meat with a slotted spoon and add to the ground meat mixture. Combine the cornstarch and cream and add to the meat mixture with the eggs and rum. Mix well.

Grease a terrine with pork fat or lard and fill with the meat mixture, pressing down well. Arrange the bay leaves and thyme on top and place in a roasting pan. Pour boiling water into the roasting pan to come about halfway up the sides of the terrine and cook in the oven for 1 hour, then cover with a lid, and cook for 1 hour more.

Remove the terrine from the roasting pan and let cool, then store in a cool place for 24 hours before serving.

Dried fruit terrine

PREPARATION TIME: 45 MINUTES
COOKING TIME: 2¼ HOURS

MAKES 3¼ POUNDS

1½ tablespoons sweet butter
4 onions, sliced
2¼ pounds boneless arm shoulder of wild boar
 (or domestic picnic ham)
1½ pounds fresh pork belly
4 teaspoons salt
a pinch of ground mild red chili powder
a pinch of ground cinnamon
scant ½ cup white port or sherry
3 tablespoons plum brandy or fruit schnapps
scant ½ cup heavy cream
3 tablespoons chopped hazelnuts
3 tablespoons chopped pistachio nuts
3 tablespoons chopped almonds
5 prunes, pitted and chopped
5 dried apricots, pitted and chopped
1 fresh thyme sprig
1 fresh rosemary sprig

Preheat the oven to 250°F. Melt the butter in a skillet. Add the onions and cook over low heat, stirring occasionally, for about 8 minutes until softened and lightly colored.

Cut ½ pound of the wild boar and ½ pound of the pork belly into cubes. Coarsely grind the remaining boar and pork. Mix together all the ingredients, except the herbs, in a large bowl.

Spoon the mixture into a terrine, pressing down well, and top with the thyme and rosemary. Place the terrine in a roasting pan and add boiling water to the pan to come about halfway up the sides of the terrine. Cook in the oven for 2 hours.

Remove the terrine from the roasting pan and let cool, then store in a cool place for 24 hours before serving.

`Back from the hunt' wild boar casserole

PREPARATION TIME: 20 MINUTES
COOKING TIME: 2 HOURS

SERVES 6

4 tablespoons olive oil
2¼ pounds boneless arm shoulder of wild boar
  (or domestic picnic ham), cut into 2-inch cubes
2 onions, sliced
1 tablespoon all-purpose flour
4 cups Côtes du Rhône or Shiraz wine
2 garlic cloves
3 shallots, halved
1 teaspoon Quatre-Épices (see page 154)
1 beef bouillon cube
⅓ cup sweet butter
1 pound 2 ounces porcini mushrooms
11 ounces chanterelle mushrooms
11 ounces cooked chestnuts

Heat the olive oil in a large, flameproof casserole. Add the wild boar and onions and cook over medium heat, stirring frequently, for about 10 minutes, until evenly browned. Stir in the flour and cook, stirring constantly, for 2–4 minutes, until golden. Stir in the red wine and add the garlic, shallots, and spice.

Mix the bouillon cube with 2¼ cups boiling water in a pitcher, add to the casserole, and bring back to a boil. Lower the heat and simmer for 1½ hours, until the meat is very tender.

Remove the meat with a slotted spoon and keep warm. Bring the cooking liquid back to a boil and cook until reduced and syrupy. Beat in 4 tablespoons of the butter.

Meanwhile, melt the remaining butter in a nonstick pan. Add both types of mushrooms and the chestnuts and cook over high heat, stirring occasionally, for about 5 minutes.

Place the wild boar in a warm dish, add the mushrooms and chestnuts, and pour the sauce over them. Serve immediately.

Jugged wild boar
with spelt and saffron risotto

PREPARATION TIME: 45 MINUTES
COOKING TIME: 1¾ HOURS

SERVES 6

2¼ pounds boneless arm shoulder of wild boar
  (or domestic picnic ham), cut into 2-inch cubes
generous ½ cup chopped fresh pork belly
4 cups Côtes du Rhône or Shiraz wine
2 shallots, sliced
3 garlic cloves, sliced
2 bay leaves
1 leek, sliced
1 bouquet garni
1 beef bouillon cube
14 ounces spelt or farro
2 onions, sliced
¼ cup sweet butter
scant 1 cup heavy cream
a pinch of saffron threads
⅔ cup grated Parmesan cheese

Put the wild boar and pork belly into a large, flameproof casserole and cook over medium heat, stirring frequently, until evenly browned. Add the red wine, shallots, garlic, bay leaves, leek, and bouquet garni. Mix the bouillon cube with 2¼ cups boiling water in a pitcher, add it to the casserole, and bring to a boil. Lower the heat and simmer for 1½ hours, until the meat is very tender.

Meanwhile, put the spelt and onions into a pan, add water to cover, and bring to a boil. Lower the heat and simmer for 45 minutes, adding more boiling water if necessary.

When the meat is tender, remove it from the casserole with a slotted spoon, and keep warm. Remove and discard the bay leaves and bouquet garni. Bring the cooking liquid back to a boil and cook until reduced and syrupy. Beat in the butter.

When the spelt is tender, cook until the water has evaporated, then stir in the cream and saffron. Cook over low heat for 5 minutes, then stir in the Parmesan. Arrange the wild boar in a serving bowl with the risotto in the center. Spoon the sauce over them and serve.

wild boar with Muscatel butter

PREPARATION TIME: 30 MINUTES
COOKING TIME: 20 MINUTES

SERVES 6

3 black radishes or turnips, thinly sliced into rounds
¼ cup sweet butter
1 teaspoon sugar
4 tablespoons olive oil
2¼ pounds boneless loin of wild boar (or boneless loin
  of domestic pork)
2¼ pounds seedless white grapes, halved
¾ cup Muscatel, white port or Sauternes wine

Put the radishes in a pan, add water to cover, 1½ teaspoons of the butter, and the sugar, and bring to a boil. Lower the heat and simmer until the water has completely evaporated and the radishes are glazed.

Heat the olive oil in a skillet. Add the wild boar and cook over high heat, turning occasionally, for about 10 minutes, until evenly browned and cooked through. Remove from the pan and keep warm.

Add the grapes to the pan, lower the heat and cook for 2 minutes, then stir in the wine, scraping up any sediment from the base of the pan with a wooden spoon. Beat in the remaining butter.

Slice the meat into thin strips and arrange randomly on individual plates with the radishes and grapes. Spoon the sauce over them and serve.

wild boar chops with tart red fruits

PREPARATION TIME: 10 MINUTES
COOKING TIME: 20 MINUTES

SERVES 6

3 crisp eating apples
2 tablespoons sweet butter
6 wild boar chops (or domestic pork chops)
4 teaspoons brandy
scant 1 cup Côtes du Rhône or Shiraz wine
¼ cup crème de cassis
½ cup gooseberries
⅓ cup dewberries or blackberries
⅔ cup raspberries

Peel and core the apples and cut them into fourths. Melt the butter in a skillet. Add the apples and cook, turning occasionally, for about 5 minutes, until golden brown. Remove from the skillet and reserve the cooking juices.

Add the chops to the skillet and cook for 5 minutes on each side, then remove from the skillet and keep warm.

Add the brandy to the skillet, heat for a few seconds, and ignite. When the flames have died down, stir in the red wine, scraping up any sediment from the base with a wooden spoon. Add the crème de cassis and cook until reduced.

Beat the reserved cooking juices into the sauce, add the fruit, and cook for 1 minute. Divide the chops and apples among individual serving plates and spoon the sauce over them.

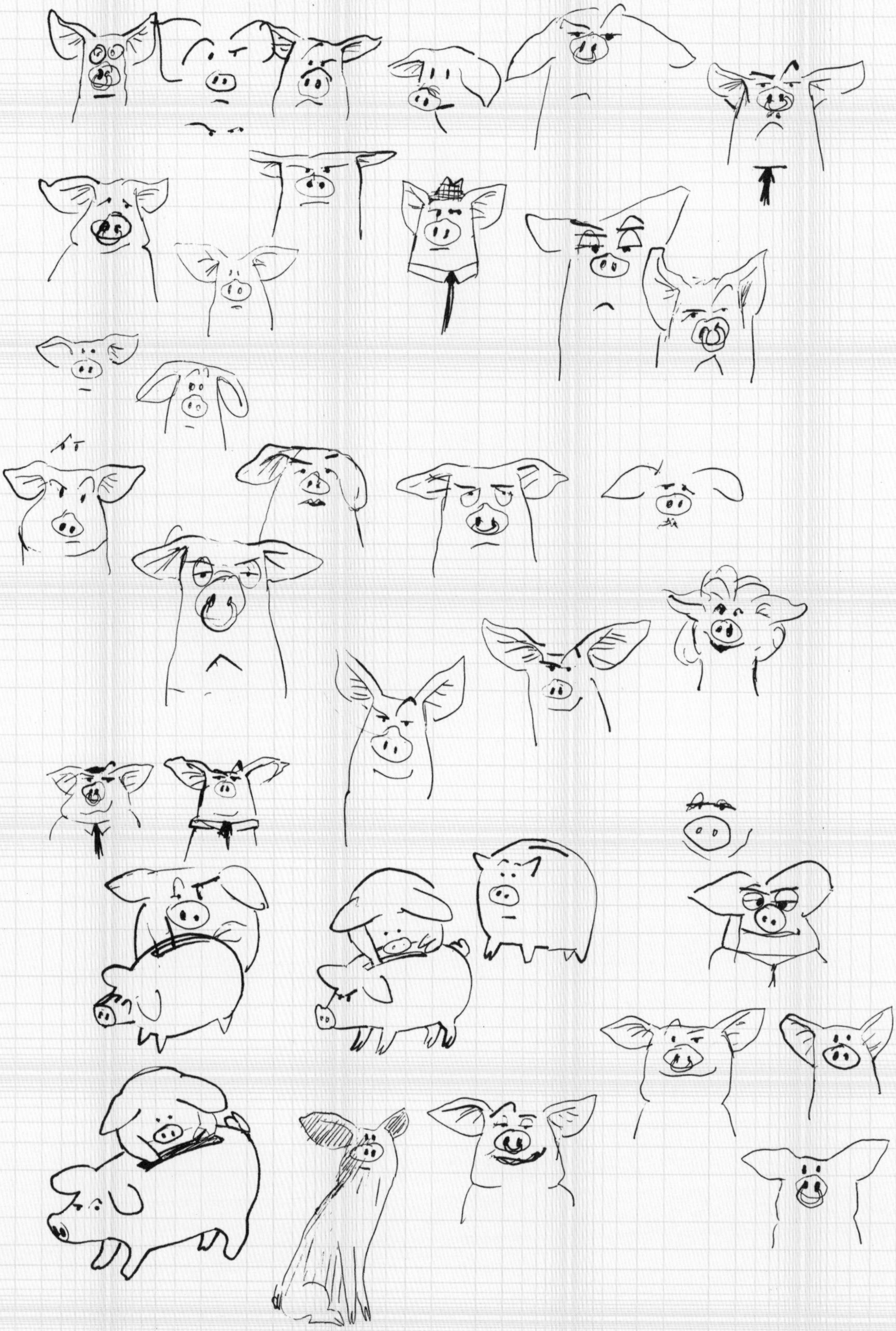

Index

TABLE OF RECIPES

INDEX

Index

CHEESES AND WINES

Cheese

Appenzeller (page 116)
Appenzeller is a semi-hard cow's milk cheese made in Switzerland. It tastes mild, and has a nutty or fruity flavor thanks to a herbal and wine brine that is applied to the cheese while it is curing.

Comté (pages 122, 328)
Comté is a semi-hard unpasteurized cow's milk cheese made in France. It is salty and has a mild nutty flavor when young, but becomes more complex and varied with age. It is a good melting cheese.

Gruyère (pages 122, 136, 328)
Gruyère is a hard unpasteurized cow's milk cheese made in Switzerland. It has a creamy (when young), nutty, earthy flavor. It is considered a good cooking cheese because it melts well and has a flavor that doesn't overpower other ingredients.

Emmental (page 128)
Emmental is a medium-hard cow's milk cheese made in Switzerland. It has large holes and a nutty flavor, and is often used in sandwiches.

Fourme d'Ambert (page 134)
Fourme d'Ambert is a soft creamy pasteurized cow's milk cheese made in France. It has a mild light blue vein through it, and a savory, nutty flavor.

Saint-Marcellin (page 328)
Saint-Marcellin is a soft creamy unpasteurized cheese made from cow's or goat's milk. It tastes slightly yeasty and has a very rustic nutty flavor.

Saint-Moret (page 116)
Saint-Moret is a cream cheese made in France.

Sarrassou (page 236)
Sarrassou is a white French cheese best described as half way between cottage cheese and yoghurt.

Wine

Beaujolais (page 156)
Beaujolais is a historical wine-producing region in France, just north of Lyon. Wines from Beaujolais are primarily red and are made from the Gamay grape. They are traditionally light, fruity, dry wines that can be drunk early.

Burgundy (page 162)
Burgundy (or Bourgogne) is the name given to white and red wines made in the Burgundy region of France. The red wines are usually made with Pinot Noir and Gamay grapes, and the white wines with Chardonnay grapes. The quality of wines from Burgundy varies dramatically; and the name Burgundy is also sometimes used outside France to describe inexpensive (or table) red wine.

Chardonnay (page 162)
The Chardonnay grape is versatile and easy to grow, and is harvested all around the world. As a result, these white wines vary greatly in flavor, but they are often soft and fruity when young and develop vanilla and caramel flavors as they age.

Côtes du Rhône (pages 232, 250, 260, 344, 348, 350, 354)
The Côtes du Rhône AC is one of the official wine-making areas within the wider Rhône region of France and includes vineyards in both the north and the south. Most Côtes du Rhône wines are red and are made from Grenach Noir, Shiraz (Syrah), Carignan, Counoise and Mourvedre grapes. Traditionally quite heavy wines, Côte du Rhône reds have recently become lighter and fruitier.

Mâcon (page 82)
Mâcon wines come from the Mâconnais part of Burgundy, France. They are light wines that should be drunk early. The red wines are predominantly made from Gamay Noir and Pinot Noir grapes, and the white wines come from Pinot Blanc and Chardonnay grapes.

Muscatel (pages 168, 84, 352)
Is a sweet fortified dessert wine made from the Muscat species of grapes, which are grown all around the world.

Riesling (pages 240, 242, 324)
Riesling is a type of white grape grown historically in France, Germany and Italy. Wines made from Riesling grapes have a spicy, fruity flavor and range from dry to sweet.

Saint Joseph (page 276)
Saint Joseph is an area in the Rhône region of France that produces mostly red wines. These are predominantly made from Shiraz (Syrah) grapes, and are considered by the locals to be resemble Beaujolais.

Shiraz (pages 232, 250, 260, 276, 344, 348, 350, 354)
Shiraz, otherwise known as Syrah, is a high-quality grape that is used to make red wine. Almost always full-bodied, the flavor of Shiraz wines does vary, but young Shiraz wines are generally rich in color, with strong spice and pepper flavors. As they mature they become more earthy and develop flavors of sweet blackberries, black currants and plums. Shiraz wines can often be a blend of more than one grape type.

Vin jaune (page 258)
Vin jaune is a white wine made in the Jura region of France from late-harvest Savagnin grapes. During production, the wine undergoes a process similar to that when making sherry, and the result is a sherry-like, delicate, nutty wine that ages extremely well and can be matured for decades.

SOURCES: PIGGY PEOPLE WE LIKE...

FRANCE

Teyssier Verdun
Place de Verdun
07320 Saint Agrève
Tel. 04 75 30 14 22

Salaison Pichon
Le Bourg
43290 Raucoules
Tel. 04 71 59 92 76

Les produits d'Auvergne chez Teil
6 rue de Lappe
75011 Paris
Tel. 01 47 00 41 28

C.C.A. La Charcuterie Alsacienne
196 rue de Vaugirard
75015 Paris
Tel. 01 45 66 87 38

Charcuterie Sibilia
102 cours Lafayette
69003 Lyon
Tel. 04 78 62 36 28

Charcuterie Bonnard
36 rue Grenette
69002 Lyon
Tel. 04 78 42 19 63

Gast
102 cours Lafayette
69003 Lyon
Tel. 04 78 62 32 25

Andouillette Duval
171 rue de la Convention
75015 Paris
Tel. 01 45 30 14 08

Andouilles Rivalan Quidu
5 rue de Bellevue
56160 Guéméné sur Scorff
Tel. 02 97 51 21 10

Andouillerie de la vallée de la Sienne
Les Planches
50450 Saint Denis le Gast
Tel. 02 33 61 44 20

Treo
112 rue des Dames
75017 Paris
Tel. 01 44 69 94 03

Jabugo Iberico & co
11 rue Clément Marot
75008 Paris
Tel. 01 47 20 03 13

Bellota-Bellota
18 rue Jean Nicot
75007 Paris
Tel. 01 53 59 96 96

S.E.E. Pléchot
11 rue Maréchal Foch
65500 Vic en Bigorre
Tel. 05 62 96 86 72

Salaisons Pyrénéennes
2 rue Anatole France
65320 Borderes sur l'Echez
Tel. 05 62 37 00 01

Pierre Oteiza
Route d'Urepel
64430 Aldudes
Tel. 05 59 37 56 11

Montauzer
Quartier Bourgade
64520 Guiche
Tel. 05 59 56 84 04

Jean-Philippe Darrieumerlou
43 rue Carnot
40800 Aire sur l'Adour
Tel. 05 58 71 77 28

De Louche à Taie
4, place Souvenir
33125 Louchats
Tel. 05 56 88 51 40

Charcuterie Blaise
28 rue du Général-de-Gaulle
29590 Le Faou
Tel. 02 98 81 91 51

Charcuterie Besançon
1 rue Fret
29160 Lanvéoc
Tel. 02 98 27 50 54

Charcuterie Léon
10 rue Saint Yves
29290 Saint Renan
Tel. 02 98 84 21 47

Pierre Schmidt
36 Grand'rue
67000 Strasbourg
Tel. 03 88 32 39 63

Porcus
6 place Temple Neuf
67000 Strasbourg
Tel. 03 88 23 19 38

Tempé Gustave & fils
68 route de Soultz
68200 Mulhouse
Tel. 03 89 52 32 33

Bouheret
26 rue Fauche
25500 Morteau
Tel. 03 81 67 10 39

**Decreuse Salaison
du Haut Doubs**
Lieu-dit La Cluse
25300 La Cluse et Mijoux
Tel. 03 81 69 55 00

*For those who live
near the spanish border:*

Chez Peïo
Dantxaria

Charcuterias y embutidos
'El Sedentario'
Camping/dancing El Faro
Hondarribia Guipuzcoa (Fontarabie)

UNITED STATES OF AMERICA

French and American cuts of meat and meat products are different, but for each recipe we have provided a suitable local equivalent. These ingredients are either available by special order from butchers in major cities or from specialty retailers online (see below). In addition, specialty grocers, such as Dean & Deluca and Whole Foods, often stock hard-to-find items.

New York

Calabria Pork Store
2338 Arthur Avenue
Bronx, NY 10458
Tel. (718) 367 5145

Cangiano Pork Stores Incorporated
6508 14th Avenue
Brooklyn, NY 11219
Tel. (718) 236 3363

Faicco's
260 Bleecker Street
New York, NY 10014
Tel. (212) 243 1974
also 6511 11th Avenue
Brooklyn
Tel. (718) 236 0119

For Italian sweet sausage.

Lobel's of New York
1096 Madison Avenue
New York, NY 10028
Tel. (877) 783 4512

Ottomanelli & Sons
285 Bleecker Street
New York, NY 10014
Tel. (212) 675 4217
www.wildgamemeatsrus.com

For wild boar.

Schatzies Prime Meats
1200 Madison Avenue
New York, NY 10128
Tel. (212) 410 1555

Vincents Meat Market
2374 Arthur Avenue
Bronx, NY 10458
Tel. (718) 295 9048

Chicago, IL

Bornhofen Meat Market
6155 N Broadway Street
Chicago, 60660
Tel. (773) 764 0714

Gepperth's Meat Market
1964 N Halsted
Chicago, IL 60614
Tel. (773) 549 3883
Fax (773) 549 3897
www.gepperthsmarket.com

Jerry and John's Quality Meats
3706 Dempster Street
Chicago, 60076
Tel. (847) 677 9360

Paulina Market
3501 N Lincoln Avenue
Chicago, 60657
Tel. (773) 248 6272
www.paulinameatmarket.com

For a complete selection of meats, including beef, pork, lamb, veal, chicken, homemade salamis, veal bratwursts and smoked pork tenderloins.

Peoria Packing & Butcher Shop
1300 West Lake
Chicago, IL 60607
Tel. (312) 738 1800

Stock Yards
340 N Oakley Boulevard
PO Box 12450
Chicago, IL 60612-0450
Tel. (800) 621 3687
Fax (312) 733 1746

Los Angeles

Best Imports
3315 Griffith Avenue
Los Angeles CA
Tel. (323) 232 6788

Eastern Meats & Deli
8320 Alondra Boulevard
Paramount, CA 90723
Tel. (562) 630 2802

Huntington Meats
6333 West 3rd Street
Los Angeles, CA 90036
Tel. (323) 938 5383
www.huntingtonmeats.com

Sunny Meat Incorporated
2801 Whittier Boulevard
Los Angeles, CA 90023
Tel. (323) 261 6788

San Francisco

Angus Meat Outlet
3450 3rd Street
San Francisco, CA 94124
Tel. (415) 824 3100

Bryan's Meats
3473 California Street
San Francisco, CA 94118
Tel. (415) 752 3430

Drewes Brothers Meat
1706 Church Street
San Francisco, CA
Tel. (415) 821 0515
www.drewesbros.com

Little City Market
1400 Stockton Street
San Francisco, CA 94133
Tel. (415) 986 2601

Piedmont Grocery Company
4038 Piedmont Avenue
Oakland, CA 94611
Tel. (510) 653 8181

Washington, DC

Canales Quality Meats
225 7th Street SE
Washington, DC 20003
Tel. (202) 547 0542

Elys Meats
1309 5th Street NE
Washington, DC 20002
Tel. (202) 544 5143

Murrays Country Meats
1309 5th Street NE
Washington, DC 20002
Tel. (202) 546 8541

Union Meat Company
225 7th Street SE
Washington, DC 20003
Tel. (202) 547 2626

Wagshal's Market
4845 Massachusetts Avenue NW
Washington, DC
Tel. (202) 363 0777

Ziggys Finest
35 New York Avenue NE
Washington, DC 20002
Tel. (202) 529 8500

Sources

Philadelphia, PA

Bennys Meat Market
6017 Torresdale Avenue
Philadelphia, PA 19135
Tel. (215) 289 6454

**Cannuli Bros. Quality
Meat and Poultry**
937 to 939 S 9th Street
Philadelphia, PA 19147
Tel. (215) 922 2988 or (215) 925 4376
Fax (215) 923 4827
www.cannulismeats.com

Cappuccios Meats
1019 S 9th Street
Philadelphia, PA 19147
Tel. (215) 922 5792

Dangelo Bros
909 S 9th Street
Philadelphia, PA 19147
Tel. (215) 923 5637
www.dangelosbros.com

For wild boar and specialty cuts and sausages.
Mail order available.

DiBruno Bros
930 S 9th Street
Philadelphia, PA 19147
Tel. (888) 322 4337
www.dibruno.com

For a wide selection of imported cheeses and
cured meats.

Dutch Country Meats
Reading Terminal Market
Philadelphia, PA 19107
Tel. (215) 922 5842

**Wilson Famous
Blue Ribbon Meats**
5694 Rising Sun Avenue
Philadelphia, PA 19120
Tel. (215) 722 2800

Baltimore, MD

Regan's Meats (Lexinton Market)
Tel. (410) 685 4563

For a selection of corned pork products
and salt pork.

Online shops

www.aidells.com
Aidells Sausages are widely available in grocers
throughout the country and the website has
a store locator. For smoked Mexican–American
style chorizo.

www.allenbrothers.com
Allen Brothers Inc.
3737 S Halsted Street
Chicago, IL 60609-1689
Tel. (800) 957 0111

www.amigofoods.com
Miami
Tel. (800) 627 2544

For Serrano ham and Spanish chorizo.

www.dangelobros.com
For Spanish chorizo.

www.dartagnan.com
Tel. (800) 327 8246

D'Artagnan meats and charcuterie are available
in gourmet shops throughout the country. For
salt pork, saucisson sec, foie gras, glace de veau,
suckling pig, wild boar, and garlic sausages.

www.dufourpastrykitchens.com
Tel. (800) 439 1282

For puff pastry, also available at Whole Foods.

www.enjoyfoiegras.com
The website of Mirepoix USA:
2342 Shattuck Ave #135
Berkeley, CA 94704
Tel. (510) 590 6693

For blood sausage, andouillette, saucisse de
Toulouse, Morteau sausage, and chipolatas.

www.fabriquesdelices.com
Tel. (703) 532 2611

For andouillettes, blood sausage, saucisse
de Toulouse, chipolatas, Morteau sausages,
foie gras, and Spanish chorizo.

www.grassorganic.com/pork.html
Ralph and Kimberlie Cole
West Wind Farms
155 Shekinah Way
Deer Lodge, Tennessee 37726
Tel. (423) 965 3334

www.heritagefoodsusa.com/index.html
Heritage Foods USA
PO Box 827
New York, NY 10150
Tel. (212) 980 6603

www.igourmet.com
Tel. (877) 446 8763

For saucisson à l'ail, chipolatas, fromage blanc,
Rosette de Lyon, saucisson sec, Spanish chorizo,
sopressata, cotechino, zampone, and piment
d'Espelette.

www.ingredientsgourmet.com
Tel. (636) 250 8394

For anchovies in salt, serrano ham, Spanish
chorizo, green peppercorns, and speck.

www.kalustyans.com
Tel. (212) 685 3451

Famous New York importer with a large
selection of grains, beans, and spices such as
brown coco beans, ras el hanout, quatre-épices
and spelt.

www.latienda.com
Williamsburg, Virginia
Tel. (800) 710 4304

For Spanish chorizo and butifarra, Serrano ham,
and piquillo peppers.

www.marcelethenri.com
San Francisco
Tel. (800) 227 6436

For poitrine roulée, andouillettes, garlic
sausage, blood sausage, and Toulouse sausage.

www.mybutcher.com
9100A Carothers Parkway, Suite 104
Franklin, TN 37067
Info@MyButcher.com

www.nimanranch.com
Niman Ranch
1025 E 12th Street
Oakland, CA 94606
Tel. (866) 808 0340
Fax (510) 808 0339
info@nimanranch.com

For caul fat, pork belly with or without rind,
uncured bacon, slab bacon, and fat back. Some
products are available at Whole Foods grocers.

www.usinger.com
Milwaukee
Tel. (800) 558 9998

For summer sausage.

www.vbutterandcheese.com
Vermont Butter & Cheese
PO Box 95
Websterville, VT 05678
Tel. (800) 884 6287

Products are also widely available in gourmet
grocers. For crème fraiche and fromage blanc.

Author's acknowledgements

For my shepherdess and my little chickens, Jean, Zoé, Basile

With many thanks to Nicoco for putting up with me.

Thanks to my whole team for letting me hog their attention morning, noon and night.

Thanks to Marie-Pierre for her talent with the camera, to José for reviving the pig, to Emanuel and his dream team for their confidence in me.

Thanks to Saint-Agrève for my healthy red cheeks...

A note about the book

Many of the recipes in this book contain raw egg, soft unpasteurized cheese, or uncooked and processed meats. These foods may have health implications for the very young, elderly or ill, or for pregnant women. Please read the recipes carefully and if in doubt contact your doctor for advice.

Phaidon Press Inc.
180 Varick Street
New York, NY 10014

www.phaidon.com

First published in English 2007
© 2007 Phaidon Press Limited

ISBN 978 0 7148 4790 0 (US edition)

First published in French by Marabout (Hachette Livre) as *Cochon & Fils*.
© 2005 Marabout (Hachette Livre)

A CIP catalogue record for this book is available from the British Library.

Hand-written titles: *Carlotta*

English edition layouts by Sandra Zellmer

Printed in China